Two Children Are Threatened by a Nightingale. 1924. Oil on wood with wood construction, 18×13″. The Museum of Modern Art, New York

max ernst

edited by William S. Lieberman

THE MUSEUM OF MODERN ART, NEW YORK

Distributed by Doubleday & Company, Inc., Garden City, New York

Exhibition dates:

The Museum of Modern Art, New York: March 1—May 7, 1961

The Art Institute of Chicago: June 16—July 23, 1961

ⓒ The Museum of Modern Art, New York, 1961

Library of Congress Catalogue Card Number 61-11269

Designed by Charles Oscar

Printed in the U.S.A.

CONTENTS

ACKNOWLEDGMENTS

On behalf of the Trustees of the Museum of Modern Art and the Art Institute of Chicago, I should like to thank first, Max Ernst and his wife Dorothea Tanning for their invaluable cooperation in the preparation of the exhibition which is recorded in this volume and, second, the generous lenders who are listed on the opposite page.

I also wish to express particular gratitude to the following persons: Mr. and Mrs. Joseph Slifka in New York have encouraged the exhibition since its inception as has Mr. Roland Penrose in London. Mr. and Mrs. J. de Menil in Houston, Mr. and Mrs. William N. Copley and M. Claude Hersaint in Paris have also been of great assistance. On behalf of the Trustees of both museums, I should also like to thank the following: Mr. James W. Alsdorf; Lord Amulree; Mr. Heinz Berggruen; Mr. Leigh B. Block; Princess de Broglie; Baron de Chollet; Mr. Richard L. Feigen; M. Robert Giron, Director General of the Société Auxiliaire des Expositions du Palais des Beaux Arts; Miss Peggy Guggenheim; Mr. Alexander Iolas; Mr. Brooks Jackson; Mr. Sidney Janis; Mrs. E. Powis Jones; Mrs. William B. Jones; Comtesse de Kermaingant; M. and Mme Jacques Lazard; Mr. Julien Levy; Mr. Alexander Liberman; M. Edouard Loeb; Mr. Allan McNab, Director of Administration at the Art Institute of Chicago; Mr. David Mann; Mr. Freddy Mayor; Mr. John Maxon, Director of Fine Arts at the Art Institute of Chicago; Miss Lee Miller; Miss Margaret Miller; M. A. D. Mouradian; Mr. John S. Newberry; Mrs. Betty Parsons; Mr. and Mrs. Bernard J. Reis; Dr. Henry M. Roland; Baron Elie de Rothschild; Dr. Haide Russell, Cultural Attaché of the German Consulate; Mme Maja Sacher-Stehlin; Mr. and Mrs. Joseph R. Shapiro; Mr. and Mrs. David M. Solinger; M. and Mme J. B. Urvater; Mr. Patrick Waldberg; M. Christian Zervos. Mr. Richard Franke in Württemberg, Mr. Michael Hertz in Bremen, and Dr. Heinz Köhn, Director of the Folkwang Museum in Essen have facilitated loans.

I wish, also, to acknowledge the help of many colleagues at the Museum of Modern Art. Mr. Alfred H. Barr, Jr., Director of the Museum Collections of the Museum of Modern Art, has granted me time from my responsibilities as Curator of Prints and Drawings and has advised me often. Mr. Bernard Karpel, the Museum's Librarian, has placed at my disposal his knowledge of the artist's work. In addition, among the Trustees and staff of the Museum, The Honorable and Mrs. William A. M. Burden, Miss Dorothy Dudley, Mr. René d'Harnoncourt, Mrs. Frederic W. Hills, Miss Elaine Johnson, Miss Alicia Legg, Mrs. Gertrud Mellon, Mrs. Clare Noble, Mr. James Thrall Soby and Mr. Monroe Wheeler have helped at many stages. Mr. Wilder Green has designed the sequence of galleries which occupy the third floor of the Museum.

Finally, I should like to thank Miss L. Lippard for research and for her translation of the prose poem "The Forest" (page 17), which first appeared in the periodical *Minotaure*.

WILLIAM S. LIEBERMAN
Director of the Exhibition

NOTE: Photographs, under the supervision of Miss Pearl Moeller, are for the most part by George Barrows, Soichi Sunami, Marc Vaux and Michel Waldberg.

LENDERS TO THE EXHIBITION

M. and Mme Jean Arp, Meudon, Seine-et-Oise; Mrs. Alfred H. Barr, Jr., New York; Mr. and Mrs. E. A. Bergman, Chicago; Mr. and Mrs. Leigh B. Block, Chicago; Jacques Bolle, Brussels; Mr. and Mrs. Raymond J. Braun, New York; Marechal Brown, Villanova, Pennsylvania; Mme Simone Collinet, Paris; Mr. and Mrs. William N. Copley, Longpont-sur-Orge, Seine-et-Oise; James Ducellier, Carcassonne, Aude; Mr. and Mrs. Marcel Duchamp, New York; Mr. and Mrs. Arne Horlin Ekstrom, New York; Judge and Mrs. Henry Epstein, New York; Max Ernst, Huismes, Indre-et-Loire; Eric Estorick, London; Richard L. Feigen, Chicago; M. H. Franke, Murrhardt, Württemberg, Germany; Mr. and Mrs. Stanley M. Freehling, Highland Park, Illinois; Allan Frumkin, Chicago; Mr. and Mrs. Varian Fry, Ridgefield, Connecticut; Mr. and Mrs. Ernö Goldfinger, London; Fernand C. Graindorge, Liège; Mr. and Mrs. Chaim Gross, New York; Robert Hendrickx, Brussels; Mme Hélène Hersaint, Behoust, Seine-et-Oise; Walter Read Hovey, Pittsburgh; Dieter Keller, Stuttgart-Feuerbach; Baron Léon Lambert, Brussels; M. and Mme Serge Landeau, Paris; Maurice Lefebvre-Foinet, Paris; Mr. and Mrs. Julien Levy, Bridgewater, Connecticut; John L. Loeb, Jr., New York; Wright S. Ludington, Santa Barbara, California; Marcel Mabille, Brussels; David Mann, New York; Alexander Margulies, London; Mr. and Mrs. Pierre Matisse, New York; Dr. and Mrs. Abraham Melamed, Milwaukee; François de Menil, Houston; Georges de Menil, Cambridge, Massachusetts; Mr. and Mrs. J. de Menil, Houston; Miss Philippa de Menil, Houston; A. D. Mouradian, Paris; Vicomtesse de Noailles, Paris; Bernard Penrose, Cornwall, England; Roland Penrose, London; Morris Philipson, New York; Mr. and Mrs. Bernard J. Reis, New York; Mme Jean Riboud, Paris; Dr. Henry M. Roland, Woking, Surrey, England; Dr. and Mrs. Allan Roos, San Francisco; Mr. and Mrs. George S. Rosenthal, Cincinnati; Mr. and Mrs. Kurt Seligmann, Sugar Loaf, New York; Mr. and Mrs.

Joseph R. Shapiro, Oak Park, Illinois; Mr. and Mrs. Joseph Slifka, New York; James Thrall Soby, New Canaan, Connecticut; Mr. and Mrs. David M. Solinger, New York; Miss Dorothea Tanning, Huismes, Indre-et-Loire; S. Tarica, Paris; Mr. and Mrs. Robert Thurman, Boston; John Torson, New York; Jacques Ulmann, Paris; Patrick Waldberg, Paris; Mr. and Mrs. Harold X. Weinstein, Chicago; Richard S. Zeisler, New York.

Stedelijk Museum, Amsterdam; Kunstmuseum, Basel; Folkwang Museum, Essen; Wadsworth Atheneum, Hartford, Connecticut; The Museum of Modern Art, New York; Philadelphia Museum of Art; Washington University, St. Louis.

Richard Feigen Gallery, Chicago; Galerie der Spiegel, Cologne; The Mayor Gallery Ltd., London; Roland, Browse & Delbanco, London; The Bodley Gallery, New York; Galerie Chalette, New York; Alexander Iolas Gallery, New York.

A NOTE TO THE READER: The artist in his writings and in interview with the editor is the author of the following text. As his basic autobiographical writings grew, they were frequently reprinted, re-edited and translated back and forth into English and French. They appeared first in the following periodicals: *La Révolution Surréaliste*, *This Quarter*, *Cahiers d'Art* and *View*, all listed in Mr. Karpel's severely condensed bibliography. Selections have been made from these writings which, for the present publication, the artist has revised and augmented.

Beyond Painting, a book by and about the artist edited by Robert Motherwell, contains further autobiographical comment as well as additional texts. Published by Wittenborn, Schultz in 1948 it remains the most important survey on the artist in English and its bibliography, compiled by Mr. Karpel, lists all writings by the artist as of its date of publication.

Max Ernst, by Patrick Waldberg, the most complete account of his life, was written in close association with the artist and published in French by Jean-Jacques Pauvert, Paris, in 1958. A year later, on the occasion of his retrospective exhibition at the Musée d'Art Moderne in Paris, the artist contributed some additional information to the compiler of its catalogue, Mme Gabrielle Vienne.

To the artist's "informal life as told by himself" printed here, the editor has added occasional notes which appear in square brackets. Italics are used when the artist speaks in the first person. "Cat. no." refers to the catalogue listing of works in the exhibition which begins on page 51; "Bibl." refers to the bibliography which begins on page 61.

AN INFORMAL LIFE OF M.E. (as told by himself to a young friend)

1891

First contact with the sensible world: On the second of April at 9:45 a.m. Max Ernst hatched from the egg which his mother had laid in an eagle's nest and over which the bird had brooded for seven years.

It happened in Brühl, six miles south of Cologne. There Max grew up and became a beautiful child. Although marked by some dramatic incidents, his childhood was not particularly unhappy.

In Cologne, at the time of Diocletian, eleven thousand virgins had surrendered their lives rather than their chastity. Their gracious skulls and bones embellish the walls of the convent church in Brühl, the very same place where little Max was forced to spend the most boring hours of his childhood. It may be that their companionship was helpful.

The geographic, political and climatic conditions of Cologne as a city are perhaps propitious to the creation of fertile conflicts in a sensitive child's mind. Many of the important crossroads of European culture meet: influences of the early Mediterranean, Western rationalism, Eastern inclination towards the occult, myths of the North, the Prussian categorical imperative, the ideals of the French Revolution, and so forth. (The continuous and powerful drama of these contradictory tendencies can be recognized in M.E.'s work. One day, perhaps, elements of a new mythology will spring from this drama.)

[Parents: Louise Kopp and Philipp Ernst, the latter a painter as well as a teacher at the School for the Deaf and Dumb for the Rhine province, in Brühl.]

1894

First contact with painting: The child watched the father at work on a small watercolor entitled *Solitude* which represented a hermit, seated in a beech forest, reading a book. Something both peaceful and menacing emanated from this *Solitude*—perhaps because of the subject (unusual in spite of its simplicity) or because of the way in which it was treated. Each of the countless leaves, stirred by branches of the tree, had been delineated with obsessive solicitude; each seemed endowed with a separate and solitary life. In the painting the hermit appeared seated somewhere beyond this world and his supernatural air both thrilled and frightened little Max. Even the very sound of the word "hermit" as pronounced by the father disturbed the child, who repeated the syllables in awkward intonations until all sense disappeared.

Max never forgot the enchantment and terror he felt when, for the first time a few days later, the father led him into the forest. (Echoes of this feeling can be found in many of M.E.'s own *Forests*, *Visions*, *Suns* and *Nights*.)

1896

First contact with drawing: Little Max made a series of drawings. They represented the father, mother, sister Maria (one year older than himself), two younger sisters, a friend and the station master of the railroad. In the sky—a train, abundantly smoking.

When asked, "What will you be when you grow up?" he always answered, "a railroad station master." Maybe the child was seduced by the nostalgia evoked by passing trains, or by the great mystery of telegraph wires which move when watched from a moving train yet stay still when you stand still.

One night, to explore the mystery of telegraph wires (and also to flee from the father's tyranny), five-year-old Max escaped from his parents' house. Blond, blue-eyed and curly-haired, he joined (by chance) a procession of pilgrims. Enchanted by the apparition of this charming child, the pilgrims proclaimed him "little Jesus Christ." To appease his father's wrath (the next day when a policeman brought him home) little Max declared he *was* the Christ Child. This candid remark inspired the father to paint a portrait of little son as little Jesus.

1897

First contact with nothingness: His sister Maria kissed him and her sisters goodbye and, a few hours later, died. After this the feeling of nothingness and the powers of destruction were utmost in his mind, in his behavior and, later, in his work.

First contact with hallucination: Measles and powers of destruction. A fever vision: *I see before me a panel crudely painted with large black strokes on a red background imitating the grain of mahogany and provoking associations of organic forms—a threatening eye, a long nose, the enormous head of a bird with thick black hair, and so forth. In front of the panel a shiny black man makes slow, comic and, according to the memories of a time long past, joyously obscene gestures. This odd fellow wears my father's moustaches. After several leaps in slow motion which revolt me, legs spread, knees folded, torso bent, he smiles and takes from his pocket a big crayon made from some soft material which I cannot more precisely describe. He sets to work. Breathing loudly he hastily traces black lines on the imitation mahogany. Quickly he gives it new, surprising and despicable forms. He exaggerates the resemblance to ferocious and viscous animals to such an extent that they become alive, inspiring me with horror and anguish. Satisfied with his art, the man seizes and gathers his creations into a kind of vase which, for this purpose, he paints in the air. He whirls the contents of the vase by moving his crayon faster and faster. The vase ends up by spinning and becomes a top. The crayon becomes a whip. Now I realize that this strange painter is my father. With all his might he wields the whip and accompanies his movements with terrible gasps of breath, blasts from an enormous and enraged locomotive. With a passion that is frantic, he makes the top jump and spin around my bed.*

Certainly little Max took pleasure in being frightened by these somnolescent visions and later voluntarily provoked hallucinations of the same kind by looking at wood panelings, clouds, wallpapers, unplastered walls, and so forth, to release his imagination. When asked, "What is your favorite occupation?" he always answered "seeing."

1898

Second contact with painting: He watched the father begin a picture in the garden *après nature* and finish it in his studio. The father omitted a tree which disturbed the composition. When he had finished the painting he went out and chopped down the tree so that no longer would there exist any difference between nature and art. Against such strict realism revolt grew in the child's heart. He decided to direct himself towards a more equitable conception of the relationship between the subjective and the objective world.

Duties at school were already odious. Indeed the very sound of the word *Pflicht* always inspired M.E. with horror and disgust. However, what the professors (of theology and ethics) named the three sources of evil—the pleasures of the eye, the pleasures of the flesh, the vanities of life—proved irresistibly attractive. (Since the cradle M.E. has neglected duties to surrender himself to the three sources of evil. Among them the pleasures of the eye have dominated.)

1906

First contact with the occult, magic and witchcraft: On the night of the fifth of January one of his closest friends, a most intelligent and affectionate pink cockatoo, died. It was a terrible shock to Max when, in the morning, he discovered the dead body and when, at the same moment, the father announced the birth of a sister.

In his imagination Max coupled these two events and charged the baby with the extinction of the bird's life. There followed a series of mystical crises, fits of hysteria, exaltations and depressions. A dangerous confusion between birds and humans became fixed in his mind and asserted itself in his drawings and paintings. (Later M.E. identified himself voluntarily with *Loplop, Bird Superior.* This phantom remained inseparable from another— *Perturbation, my Sister: the Hundred Headless Woman.*)

Excursions into the world of marvels, chimeras, phantoms, poets, monsters, philosophers, birds, women, lunatics, magi, trees, eroticism, poisons, mathematics, and so forth. A book that he wrote at this time the father found and burned. The title was *Divers' Manual*.

At the age of adolescence, the well-known game of purely imaginary occurrences seen in somnolescence: *A procession of men and women, attired in everyday dress, come from a distant horizon towards my bed. Before arriving, they separate: the women pass to the right, the men to the left. Curious, I lean toward the right so that not a single face will escape me. At first I am struck by the extreme youth of all these women, but, upon close examination face by face, I realize my mistake—many are middle-aged and only two or three are very young, about eighteen years old, the age convenient to my adolescence. I am too occupied with these women to pay much attention to what passes on the left. But without seeing I know that there I would make the opposite error. All these men begin to shock me because of their precocious senility and remarkable ugliness, but among them, upon close examination, only my father continues to have the features of an old man.*

1909

[Receives his baccalaureate. Plans a degree in philosophy at the University of Bonn with the intention of specializing in psychiatry.] As his family obliged Max to continue his studies, he was enrolled at the University of Bonn. He followed, however, the path on which he had embarked at the *gymnasium:* neglected duties to surrender passionately to the most gratuitous activity there is—painting.

His eyes were avid not only for the amazing world which assailed them from the exterior but also for that other world, mysterious and disquieting, which burst forth and vanished in adolescent dreams with persistence and regularity: *To see it clearly becomes a necessity for my nervous equilibrium. To see it clearly there is only one way—to record all offered to my sight.*

1910-1911

The young man, eager for knowledge, avoided any studies which might degenerate into breadwinning. Instead his pursuits were those considered futile by his professors—predominantly painting. Other futile pursuits: reading seditious philosophers and unorthodox poetry, transient pleasures, and so forth. Attracted by the most audacious spirits, he was willing to receive the most contradictory influences—in painting, for example —Manet, Gauguin, van Gogh, Goya, Macke, Kandinsky, Delaunay, and so forth.

What to do about consequent confusion? Struggle like a blind swimmer? Appeal to reason? Submit to discipline? Or, accentuate contradictions to the point of paroxysm? Should he abandon himself in his night, indulge in the luxury of losing reason? The young man's temperament predisposed him to accept the last solution.

[In the course of his studies visits asylums and, for the first time, sees the art of the insane about which he decides to write a book.] Near Bonn there was a group of sinister looking buildings resembling, in many ways, the Hospital of St. Anne in Paris. At this "clinic for the mentally ill," students could take courses and practical jobs. One of the buildings housed an astonishing collection of sculpture and paintings executed in spite of themselves by the inmates of this horrible place. These works strongly touched and troubled the young man. *I try to recognize streaks of genius in them and decide to explore fully those vague and dangerous lands confined by madness.* (But it was only much later that M.E. discovered certain processes which helped him venture into these no-man's lands.)

Meets August Macke, a subtle poet, the very image of just and intelligent enthusiasm, generosity, judgment and exuberance. [Macke, himself influenced by Robert Delaunay, lived in Bonn. With Wassily Kandinsky, Franz Marc, Alexei Jawlensky and Paul Klee, he was a member of *Der Blaue Reiter* in Munich. Macke was also associated with the group around Herwarth Walden, dealer and publisher of *Der Sturm* in Berlin, as well as with avant-garde painters and poets in France and Germany. He was killed in 1914.]

1912

[M.E. joins *Das Junge Rheinland*, a group of friends, poets and painters stimulated to a great extent by Macke.] We were filled with heroism. Spontaneity was *de rigeur*. No doctrine, no discipline, no duties to fulfill. United by a thirst for life, poetry, liberty, the absolute and knowledge. *C'était trop beau* . . . [Decides he is a painter. Sees the Cologne Sonderbund exhibition which includes van Gogh, Cézanne, Munch and Picasso. Meets Munch.]

[First exhibitions: 1912, at the informal galleries of *Das Junge Rheinland* in the bookshop of Friedrich Cohen, Bonn; at the Feldmann Gallery, Cologne; 1913, at the Gereon Club, Cologne; at the *Erst Deutsche Herbstsalon*, Berlin—the last, a group exhibition presented by *Der Sturm* and organized by Macke and Kandinsky, includes work by Chagall, Delaunay and Klee.]

1913

[Meets Guillaume Apollinaire, accompanied by Delaunay.] It was only once at Macke's house. Needless to say M.E. was deeply moved. What he had read had dazzled and excited him. "Zône" had appeared in *Der Sturm;* and the first edition of *Alcools*, published by Mercure de France with a Picasso drawing, had arrived in Cologne. We were speechless, utterly captivated by Apollinaire's winged words which flew from the lightest to the most serious, from deep emotion to laughter, from paradox to incisively accurate formulation.

First contact with Paris, the third week of August: Armed with a light suitcase arrived at the Gare du Nord, scorned the cabs, took the Boulevard de Strasbourg, then Sébastopol, slowing down at intersections, cafés, storefronts, eyes bulging, lying in wait. Arrived at Les Halles. Refreshed after a bowl of soup and a horn of *frites*, wandered around and felt right. Rented a room, Hôtel des Ducs de Bourgogne, the rue de Pont Neuf, leaned out the window, saw the Seine. (Macke had given letters; looked up no one.) Happy to wander all day in different *quartiers*. At night theaters, dance halls and cabarets. Went often to Montparnasse where, at the Café Dôme, met Jules Pascin. At the end of four weeks, money gone, had to leave. (In Paris, M.E. had experienced that feeling of *belonging* which, as Patrick Waldberg reminds us, is like love at first sight and binds forever.)

1914

First contact with Arp: One day in Cologne M.E. noticed someone about his own age in a gallery which showed works by Cézanne, Derain, Braque and Picasso. His face was handsome and spiritual, his manners courtly. However they contrasted strangely with what he was doing. With gentleness (Franciscan) and competence (Voltairian), he seriously was attempting to explain to an old fool the virtues of modern art. The imbecile pretended to be convinced but exploded with rage when Arp showed him some of his own drawings. With shouts and gestures he announced that he was seventy-two, that his whole life and strength had been devoted to art and that, if this were the result of all his sacrifices, it would be better . . . Quietly Arp suggested that it would be better—to ascend to heaven. Pronouncing maledictions the fool left; M.E. and Arp joined hands to conclude a pact of friendship still vigorous today.

On the first of August 1914 M.E. died. He was resurrected on the eleventh of November 1918 as a young man who aspired to find the myths of his time. Occasionally he consulted the eagle who had brooded the egg of his prenatal life. (You may find the bird's advice in his works.)

[War: Four years at the front as an artillery engineer. At the front twice wounded, by the recoil of a gun, by the kick of a mule. His fellow soldiers named him "the man with the head of iron." Invalided 1917. In February, M.E. and Paul Eluard, not yet acquainted, had fought on the same front, opposite sides.]

How to overcome the disgust and fatal boredom that military life and the horrors of war create? Howl? Blaspheme? Vomit? Or, have faith in the therapeutic virtues of a contemplative life? Circumstances were not favorable. However, he decided to make an attempt. A few watercolors, even paintings, (executed in moments of calm) attest this. Many of these, lost or destroyed, already contained the germ of later works (*Histoire Naturelle*, 1925). A few titles, still remembered, indicate a state of mind: *Desire of a plant to cling, Of love in the inanimate world, Descent of animals into the valley at night, A leaf unfolds*, and so forth.

1916

[DADA is born in Zurich. *Der Sturm* organizes a small exhibition of M.E.'s work in January and publishes a drawing as cover of the periodical, vol. 6, no. 19/20.]

1917

[*Der Sturm* publishes "On the Development of Color," an article by M.E., bibl. 1].

1918

[DADA arrives in Germany. M.E. marries Louise Strauss, a student of art history.]

1919

[On a trip to Munich M.E. sees DADA publications from Zurich and discovers that Arp is alive. In Munich M.E. also sees an exhibition of Klee whom he visits for the first and last time. In the magazine *Valori Plastici*, he sees the work of de Chirico and, as a result, creates the album of eight lithographs *Fiat Modes Pereat Ars* (cat. no. 234). M.E. composes his first altered engravings and collages.]

Enter, enter, have no fear of being blinded—One rainy day in 1919 in a town on the Rhine, my excited gaze is provoked by the pages of a printed catalogue. The advertisements illustrate objects relating to anthropological, microscopical, psychological,

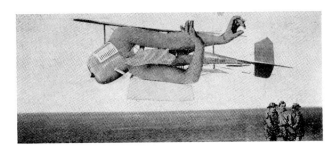

Collage. 1920. Pasted photoengravings, 2⅜ x 5⅝".
Private collection, New York.

The Swan Is Very Peaceful. 1920. Pasted photoengravings, 3¼ x 4¾". Collection Mrs. Alfred H. Barr, Jr., New York.

mineralogical and paleontological research. Here I discover the elements of a figuration so remote that its very absurdity provokes in me a sudden intensification of my faculties of sight—a hallucinatory succession of contradictory images, double, triple, multiple, superimposed upon each other with the persistence and rapidity characteristic of amorous memories and visions of somnolescence. These images, in turn, provoke new planes of understanding. They encounter an unknown—new and non-conformist. By simply painting or drawing, it suffices to add to the illustrations a color, a line, a landscape foreign to the objects represented—a desert, a sky, a geological section, a floor, a single straight horizontal expressing the horizon, and so forth. These changes, no more than docile reproductions of what is visible within me, record a faithful and fixed image of my hallucination. They

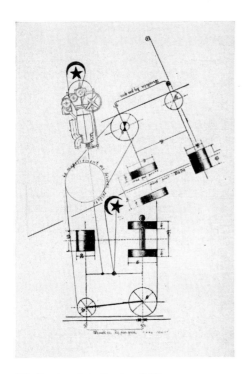

The Roaring of the Ferocious Soldiers 1919.
Printer's proof altered with pen and ink,
14⅛ x 9⅜″. The Bodley Gallery, New York.

transform the banal pages of advertisement into dramas which reveal my most secret desires.

[Dadamax Ernst and J. T. Baargeld form the DADA conspiracy in the Rhineland and, with others, a DADA center, W/3 West Stupidia. They publish *Der Ventilator*, banned by the British army of occupation, also *Bulletin D*, and arrange the first DADA exhibition in Cologne.]

1920

Der Arp ist da. [Cologne: February, first issue of *Die Schammade* edited by Dadamax and Baargeld. Arp had returned and joined them. He and M.E. produce *Fatagaga* (*fabrication de tableaux garantis gazométriques*). April: Second, culminating DADA exhibition—*DADA Ausstellung DADA Vorfrühling*. Meets Kurt Schwitters. Birth of a son, Jimmy.]

[Paris: First contact with André Breton: Dadamax is invited to exhibit his collages. In May, the exhibition opens *Au sans pareil*.]

1921

[Cologne: Eluard, accompanied by his wife Gala, visits Cologne and selects collages as illustrations to his poems. Dadamax signs *DADA soulève tout*, a DADA manifesto.]

[Tyrol: Summers at Tarrenz-bei-Imst with Arp, Sophie Taeuber, Tristan Tzara and, for the last time, Louise Ernst. Contributions, "*Dada au grand air*" to DADA Tyrol issue of DADA magazine.]

1922

[Summer: Again, in the Tyrol.] August: Born and bred in the Rhineland, escaped, with neither papers nor money, to Paris to live. [Settles in Saint Brice, a suburb near Montmorency, in the same building with Eluard. Works in an atelier which manufactures souvenirs of Paris. Publication of *Les Malheurs des Immortels*, and *Répétitions* (bibl. 10, 11), two collaborative volumes, collages by M.E., poems by Eluard.]

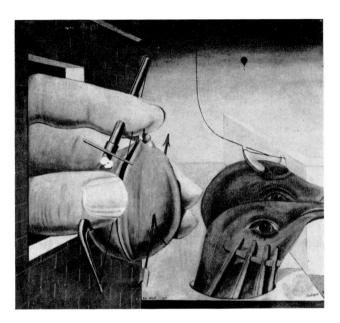

Oedipus Rex. 1922. Oil on canvas, 35 x 45¾″.
Private collection, Paris.

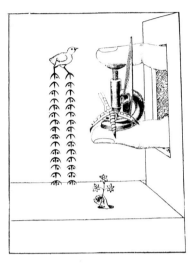

The Invention. A collage from Paul
Eluard, *Répétitions.* 1922. Bibl. 11.

1923

[Paints: *Equivocal Woman, Saint Cecelia, The Couple,* cat.
nos. 7, 8, 9 and the first version of *Woman, Old Man and
Flower.* The last, completely repainted the following year,
cat. no. 11.] The woman, of course, lies in the old man's
arm. The other figure is the flower.

1924

Two Children Are Threatened by a Nightingale [cat. no. 12],
the last in the series which started with *Elephant of the
Celebes, Oedipus Rex, Revolution by Night* [cat. nos. 3, 4, 6],
La Belle Jardinière [destroyed] and, probably, the last
consequence of his early collages—a kind of farewell to

a technique and to occidental culture. (This painting,
it may be interesting to note, was very rare in M.E.'s
work: He never imposes a title on a painting. He waits
until a title imposes itself. Here, however, the title
existed *before* the picture was painted. A few days before
he had written a prose poem which began: *à la tombée de
la nuit, à la lisière de la ville, deux enfants sont menacés par un
rossignol* . . . He did not attempt to illustrate this poem,
but that is the way it happened.)

[M.E. sells all of his work in Germany, sails in July
for the Far East. M.E., Gala and Eluard are rejoined in
Saigon. M.E. spends about three months traveling, returns via Marseilles. Breton's first Surrealist Manifesto,
issued in Paris October.] M.E. found his friends in Paris
en plein effervescence.

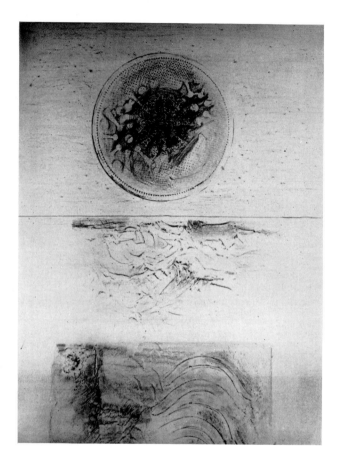

Earthquake. 1925. Pencil frottage, 24 x 18½".
The Bodley Gallery, New York.

1925

On the tenth of August (in Pornic, the home of Gilles de Laval,) M.E. found a process which rests solely upon the intensification of the mind's powers of irritability. In view of the characteristics of its technique, he called it *frottage* [rubbing] and, in his own personal development, it has had an even larger share than collage from which, indeed, he believes it does not fundamentally differ. By means of appropriate techniques, by excluding all conscious mental influences (of reason, taste or morals) and by reducing to a minimum the active part of what, until now has been called the "author," this process revealed itself as the exact equivalent of what was known as automatic writing. By enlarging the active part of the mind's hallucinatory faculties, he succeeded in attending, simply as a spectator, the birth of his works.

Enter, enter, have no fear of being blinded—One rainy day at an inn by the seaside, I discover myself recalling how in childhood the panel of imitation mahogany opposite my bed had served as the optical stimulant to visions in somnolence. Now I am impressed by the obsession imposed upon my excited gaze by the wooden floor, the grain of which had been deepened and exposed by countless scrubbings. I decide to investigate the symbolism of this obsession and, to aid my meditative and hallucinatory powers, I take from the boards a series of drawings. At random I drop pieces of paper on the floor and then rub them with black lead. By examining closely the drawings thus obtained, I am surprised at the sudden intensification of my visionary capacities.

My curiosity awakened, I marvel and am led to examine in the same way, all sorts of materials that fall into my field of vision—leaves and their veins, the ragged edges of sack cloth, the palette knife's markings on a "modern" painting, thread unrolled from its spool and so forth—that end with a kiss (the Bride of the Wind).

Drawings obtained in this way—thanks to a progression of suggestions and transmutations which occur spontaneously (like hypnagogical visions)—lost the character of the material employed, here for example wood, and assumed the aspect of unbelievably precise images which were probably able to reveal the initial cause of the obsession or to produce some semblance of its cause.

These drawings, these first fruits of frottage, were assembled as *Histoire Naturelle* from *The Sea and the Rain* to *Eve, the Only One Left.* [Their titles]: *The Sea and the Rain— A Glance—Little tables around the earth—Shawl of Snow Flakes—Earthquake—Pampas—He will fall far from here— False Positions—Confidences—She guards her secret—Whip lashes or lava threads—Fields of Honor, Inundations, Seismic Plants—Scarecrows—Sprint of the Chestnut Tree—Scars—The linden tree is docile—The Fascinating Cypress—Habits of Leaves—Idol—The Palette of Caesar—Huddling against the walls—Enter into the continents—Vaccinated Bread—Flashes of lightning under fourteen years old—Conjugal Diamonds— Origin of the Clock—In the stable of the sphinx—Dead Man's Meal—Wheel of Light—He who Escaped—System of Solar Money—To Forget Everything—Stallion and the Wind's Betrothed—Eve, the Only One Left.*]

At first it seemed frottage could be used only for drawings. Then M.E. adapted it to painting. It revealed a field of vision limited only by the capacity of irritability of the mind's powers.

[Many of the "natural history" frottages published as a portfolio the following year, preface by Arp, bibl. 12. Contributes to the first Surrealist group exhibition at the Galerie Pierre, Paris. Autumn: Roland Penrose sees *La Belle Jardinière* by M.E. reproduced in the magazine *La Révolution Surréaliste.* They meet.]

1926

January: I see myself lying in bed and, at my feet, standing, a tall thin woman, dressed in a very red gown. The gown is transparent, so is the woman. I am enchanted by the surprising elegance of her bone structure. I am tempted to pay her a compliment.

[M.E. and Joan Miró collaborate on the ballet *Roméo et Juliette* for Diaghilev. As a result, a broadside signed by Breton and Louis Aragon condemns them for unsurrealist activities. *Roméo et Juliette*, a ballet in two tableaux, first presented by the Ballets Russes at the Théâtre de Monte Carlo, May 4. Music by Constant Lambert; decors and costumes by M.E. and Miró; choreography by Bronia Nijinska.]

1927

[January in Megève. February returns to Paris. Meets and marries Marie-Berthe Aurenche without her parents' blessing. Paints *Young People Trampling Their Mother; Vision Provoked by a String Found on My Table; The Horde; Vision Provoked by the Nocturnal Aspects of the Porte St. Denis; One Night of Love;* cat. nos. 35, 36, 38, 42, 43].

1928

Entrance of the flowers: Aux rendez-vous des amis . . . C'était la belle saison. . . *It is the time of serpents, earthworms, feather flowers, shell flowers, bird flowers, animal flowers, tube flowers. It is the time when the forest takes wing and flowers struggle under water. (Was he not a pretty flower?) It is the time of the circumflex medusa.*

[Publication of Breton's *Le Surréalisme et la Peinture,* bibl. 36, reproducing among other works by M.E.: *The Little Tear Gland That Says Tic-Tac, Revolution by Night, Two Children Are Threatened by a Nightingale, Young People Trampling Their Mother,* cat. nos. 186, 6, 12, 35.]

1929

One day a painter asked M.E., "What are you doing now, are you working?" "Yes," he replied, "I am making collages. I am preparing a book which will be called *The Hundred Headless Woman.*"

The acquaintance whispered in his ear, "And what sort of glue are you using?" With that modest air which his contemporaries so admire, he admitted that in most of his collages, there is little use for glue; that he is not responsible for the term "collage," that of fifty-six of the catalogue numbers of his exhibition of "collages" in 1920, only twelve justified the term *collage-découpage.* As for the other forty-four, Aragon was right when he said "the place to catch the thoughts of M.E. is the place where, with a little color, a line of pencil, he ventures to

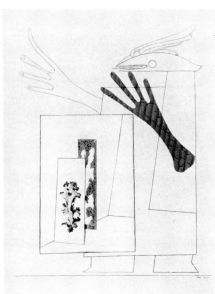

far left: *Loplop Introduces.* 1929-30. Pasted color engraving and pencil, 24½ x 19″. Collection Mr. and Mrs. E. A. Bergman, Chicago.

left: *Loplop Introduces.* 1931. Pasted paper, pencil, and crayon, 25⅜ x 19⅝″. Collection Mr. and Mrs. Julien Levy, Bridgewater, Connecticut.

acclimate the phantom which he has just precipitated into a foreign landscape." Maxim: If it is not plumes that make plumage, it is not glue [*colle*] that makes collage. [Meets Alberto Giacometti. Publication of M.E.'s collage novel *La Femme 100 têtes,* bibl. 13.]

1930

After having composed with method and violence my novel The Hundred Headless Woman, *I am visited almost daily by the Bird Superior, Loplop—my private phantom. He presents me with a heart in a cage, the sea in a cage, two petals, three leaves, a flower and a young girl. Also, the man of the black eggs and the man with the red cape.*

One beautiful autumn afternoon he relates that he had once invited a Lacedemonian to come and listen to a man who imitated perfectly the nightingale. The Lacedemonian replied, "I have often heard the nightingale itself."

One evening he tells some maxims, which don't make me laugh. Maxim: it is better not to reward a beautiful deed than to reward it badly. Illustration: A soldier lost both arms in battle. His colonel offered him a silver dollar. Said the soldier, "No doubt you think, sir, that I have lost a pair of gloves."

[The collage novel by M.E., *Rêve d'une petite fille qui voulut entrer au Carmel,* published, bibl. 14. July: The film *L'Age d'Or* by Luis Bunuel and Salvador Dali, in part inspired by M.E.'s pictures, is privately shown at the home of the Vicomte de Noailles. M.E., himself, appears in the film.]

1931

[Nine paintings by the German romantic Caspar David Friedrich, destroyed by fire while on exhibition at the Glass Palace, Munich. Patrick Waldberg describes effect of this destruction upon M.E.: "He felt the loss to the point of sickness. Beyond painting, profound spiritual ties united him—beyond time—to this poet-artist in whom his own preoccupations discovered a kindred echo. Caspar David Friedrich had said: 'Close your physical eyes in order to see first your painting with the spiritual eye. Next, bring into the daylight what you have seen in your night so that your action is exercised in turn on other beings from the exterior to the interior.' M.E. has never ceased to follow this advice."]

[First exhibition in the United States: Julien Levy Gallery, New York.]

1932

[Finishes series of collages, *Loplop introduces . . .* , begun in 1929, cat. no. 211-218a.]

1933

[In the early summer visits northern Italy: Le Roncoli, Vigoleno and Ravenna. Paints the largest of his forest pictures, cat. no. 63 and, the next year for the magazine *Minotaure*, bibl. 4, writes:]

What is a forest? A supernatural insect. A drawing board. What do forests do? They never retire early. They await the woodcutter. What is summer for the forests? The future: that will be the season when masses of shadows will be able to change themselves into words and when beings gifted with eloquence will have the nerve to seek midnight at zero o'clock.

But that is time past, it seems to me. Perhaps.

In that time past did nightingales believe in God? In that time past nightingales did not believe in God. They were bound in friendship to mystery.

And man, what position was he in? Man and the nightingale found themselves in the most favorable position for imagining: they had in the forest a perfect guide to dreams.

What is dreaming? You ask of me too much; it is a woman who fells a tree.

What are forests for? To make gifts of matches to children as toys.

Is, then, fire in the forest? Fire is in the forest.

What do the plants live on? Mystery.

What day is it? Merde.

What will be the death of the forests? The day will come when a forest, until then a friend of dissipation, will decide to frequent only sober places, tarred roads and Sunday strollers. She will live on pickled newspapers. Affected by virtue, she will correct these bad habits contracted in her youth. She will become geometric, conscientious, dutiful, grammatical, judicial, pastoral, ecclesiastical, constructivist and republican . . . It will be a bore. Will the weather be fair? Of course! We'll go on a presidential hunt.

Will the name of this forest be Blastula or Gastrula? Her name will be Mme de Rambouillet.

Will the forest be praised for her new conduct? Not by me. She will find this most unfair, and one day, unable to stand it any longer, she will dump her trash in the heart of the nightingale. What will the nightingale say to that? The nightingale will be galled. "My friend," he will reply, "You are worth even less than your reputation. Go take a trip to Oceania, you'll see."

And will she go? Too proud.

Do forests still exist there? They are, it seems, savage and impenetrable, black and russet, extravagant, secular, swarming, diametrical, negligent, ferocious, fervent and lovable, with neither yesterday nor tomorrow. From one island to another, over volcanos, they play cards with incomplete decks. Nude, they wager only their majesty and their mystery.

On the 24th of December, I am visited by a young chimera in evening dress.

1934

Eight days later I meet a blind swimmer . . . A little patience (fifteen days of waiting) and I will be present at the attirement of the bride. The bride of the wind embraces me while passing at full gallop (simple effect of touch).

[Summer: Maloja, Switzerland, with Giacometti. Sculpts in stone. Publication of *Une Semaine de Bonté, ou les sept éléments capiteaux*, bibl. 15, M.E.'s most ambitious collage novel.]

[M.E. told Roland Penrose later:] *All of these works suggest an overwhelming sense of motion through time and space. They vibrate with the incongruous and irrational qualities generally attributed to dreams although artists know they are the original breath of reality. The elements of the collages, banal engravings from old books, are metamorphosed, transformed. Birds become men and men become birds. Catastrophes become hilarious. Everything is astonishing, heartbreaking and possible.*

1935

I see barbarians looking toward the west, barbarians emerging from the forest, barbarians walking to the west. On my return to the garden of the Hesperides I follow, with joy scarcely concealed, the rounds of a fight between two bishops . . . Voracious gardens in turn devoured by a vegetation which springs from the debris of trapped airplanes . . .

With my eyes I see the nymph Echo.

1936

October: If you are to believe the description on his identity card, M.E. would be no more than forty-five when he writes these lines. He would have an oval face, blue eyes and greying hair. His height would be only slightly more than average. As for distinguishing marks of identification, this card allows him none. Consequently he could, if pursued by the police, plunge into the crowd and easily disappear forever.

Women, on the other hand, find that his young face framed by silky white hair "makes him look very distinguished." They see in him charm, a great sense of

"reality" and seduction, a perfect physique and agreeable manners (the danger of pollution, he himself admits, has become such an old habit that he is rather proud of it as a "sign of worldliness"). They find, also, a character difficult, inextricable, obstinate; also an impenetrable mind. "He is," they say, "a nest of contradictions," at once transparent and enigmatic, something like the pampas.

It is difficult for them to reconcile the gentleness and moderation of his expression with the calm violence which is the essence of his thought. They readily compare him to a gentle earthquake which does no more than rock the furniture yet does not hurry to displace everything. What is particularly disagreeable and unbearable to them is that they can almost never discover his *identity* in the flagrant (apparent) contradictions which exist between his spontaneous behavior and the dictates of his conscious thoughts. For instance, they can observe two apparently irreconcilable attitudes: first, that of the god Pan and the man Papou, who possess all the mysteries and in their interplay realize a union ("He marries nature, he pursues the nymph Echo"); and, second, that of a Prometheus, thief of fire, conscious and organized, who, guided by thought, pursues with implacable hate and gross injuries. "This monster is pleased only by the antipodes of the landscape," they say. And a teasing little girl adds, "He is, at the same time, a brain and a vegetable."

[Meets the painter Leonore Fini. Ignoring Breton's veto, M.E. participates in exhibition *Fantastic Art, Dada, Surrealism*, Museum of Modern Art, New York, autumn, 1936, with 48 works, almost twice as many as any other exhibitor.]

1937

[Publication by Cahiers d'Art of *Au delà de la Peinture*, devoted to M.E.'s work from 1918 to 1936, bibl. 21.] *I dedicate this book to Roland Penrose, to the nymph Echo and to the antipodes of the landscape.*

[Decors for *Ubu Enchaîné*, a play by Alfred Jarry

Study for the stage set for *Ubu Enchaîné.* 1937. Pasted engravings, pencil and colored crayon, 9⅝ x 13¼".
The Bodley Gallery, New York.

directed by Sylvain Itkine. First presented by the Compagnie du Diable Éclarte at the Comédie des Champs-Elysées, Paris, September 22.]

[Meets the painter Leonora Carrington.]

1938

Enraged by a monstrous demand, "to sabotage in every possible way the poetry of Paul Eluard," M.E. quit the surrealist group.

[With Leonora Carrington settles at Saint Martin d'Ardèche, near Pont St. Esprit about thirty miles north of Avignon. Decorates their home with murals and bas-reliefs. Illustrates and, with the following text, in part introduces her novella *La Maison de la Peur,* bibl. 7. Loplop speaks:]

Good wind, ill wind, I present you the Bride of the Wind . . . Who is the Bride of the Wind? Can she read? Can she write in French without making mistakes? What fuel keeps her warm? . . . She is kindled by her intensity, her mystery, her poetry. She has read nothing, yet she has drunk everything. She knows not how to

read. Nevertheless, the nightingale saw her, seated on the stone of spring, reading. And, although she read in silence, animals and horses listened rapt with admiration.

1939

[War is declared. Paints *A Moment of Calm,* cat. no. 84. Interrupted.] "He is under the jurisdiction of the German Reich." As an enemy alien, M.E. was interned: first for six weeks in a camp at Largentière, then transferred to Les Milles near Aix-en-Provence. Liberated at Christmas time, thanks to a petition by Eluard to Albert Sarrault, M.E. returned to Saint Martin. Survived on subsidies sent him by his friend Joë Bousquet.

1940

May: Interned again, first in a camp at Lorio, then transferred to the St. Nicholas (!) camp near Nîmes. Escaped to Saint Martin, recaptured, interned again, escaped again just as his papers for release arrived. Allowed to return, once more, to Saint Martin. [Now, sought by the Gestapo, M.E. begins to paint *Europe after the Rain* (cat. no. 90). Decides to leave Europe.] An offer of shelter secured in the United States by several friends including Marga Barr, son Jimmy, expedited through the Emergency Rescue Committee by Varian Fry.

1941

[On his way, at Marseille, M.E. meets Breton also seeking a way to leave. Attempt at reconciliation. Meets Peggy Guggenheim. Because of complications with his transit visa, M.E. has trouble leaving France but finally crosses the border to Madrid and leaves, with Peggy Guggenheim, from Lisbon.]

July: M.E. arrived in New York at the La Guardia airport where his son Jimmy welcomed him to the United States. From the plane he had glimpsed the lovely lady, the Statue of Liberty. Hardly off the plane he was seized by immigration authorities. "He is under the jurisdiction of the German Reich." Interned in the fortress of Ellis Island—had a splendid view of the Statue of Liberty. Liberated after three days, M.E. traveled for several weeks across the United States—Chicago, New Orleans, Arizona, New Mexico, California. [Decides to settle in New York.]

First painting in America: *Napoleon in the Wilderness* (cat. no. 91). The decalcomania base was begun in France, but the painting was finished in Santa Monica, shortly after M.E.'s arrival. (He had just quit Europe: Napoleon —the dictator; wilderness—Saint Helena; exile—defeat, and so forth. The painting, he discovered, bore a strange likeness to an allegory by Piero di Cosimo in the Kress Collection.) About a month later when M.E. visited the National Gallery in Washington, he was amazed to see the resemblance in *idea* between this picture, which he had never seen before, and his own painting—the strange horse dancing, the guardian winged female figure, the string and, in the foreground, the sea monster.

Loplop, Bird Superior, had followed the airplane which brought me to this country on the fourteenth of July, and the bird builds his nest in a cloud on the East River.

[Marries Peggy Guggenheim. They separate at the close of the following year.]

In New York, on Wall Street, M.E. enjoyed the way they pronounced his name and added it to his collection. Here it is: Mac, Maxt, Mex, Mask, Oinest, Oinst, and so forth.

1942

Exhibitions in New York, Chicago and New Orleans, complete "flops." The press hostile (or silent), the public recalcitrant (sales nil), and so forth. Compensation: Young painters and poets were enthusiastic.

In the same year, the non-Euclidian fly appears.

[At the Wakefield Bookshop, New York, Betty Parsons shows in a group exhibition a painting by M.E.] It provoked the curiosity of some of the young painters. The technique especially intrigued them. M.E. explained: It is a children's game. Attach an empty tin can to a thread a metre or two long, punch a small hole in the bottom, fill the can with paint, liquid enough to flow freely. Let the can swing from the end of the thread over a piece of canvas resting on a flat surface, then change the direction of the can by movements of the hands, arms, shoulder and entire body. Surprising lines thus drip upon the canvas. The play of association then begins.

[This particular painting, slightly altered by M.E., becomes *Young Man intrigued by the flight of a non-Euclidian fly*, now in a private collection in Zurich repr. bibl. 30, p. 61. The magazine *View* devotes an issue to M.E., bibl. 22. M.E. collaborates on the founding of the magazine *VVV*.]

1943

Within the realm of the possible, at last, a gathering. [M.E. meets the painter Dorothea Tanning. They spend the summer in Arizona.]

[Sidney Janis in his *Abstract and Surrealist Art in America* (bibl. 42), published the following year, writes: "In his American pictures, as in the past, Max Ernst continues to invent new techniques with which he creates the properties of enigma that inevitably fill his work. He has recently invented a new method of chance—oscillation—and in this technique has painted several large gyrating compositions. They are produced by means of color flowing freely from a swinging container operated with a long cord by the artist. Ernst in several recent works has combined techniques as well as images from many periods. These are compartmentalized by horizontal and vertical lines which divide them into rectangular segments somewhat resembling the spatial order of Mondrian. *Day and Night* [1942, cat. no. 94] painted previously, anticipated this trend. One of these pictures, *Vox Angelica* [1943 cat., no. 96] is an autobiographical account in episodes of dream and reality, of his peregrinations from one country to another."]

1944

Summer: M.E. found himself working steadily at sculpture. He had rented a place at Great River, Long Island, with the intention of spending the summer swimming. But there were so many mosquitoes that we could not poke our noses out of doors. Decided to take over the garage, screen it and make a studio. There he worked the summer on sculpture.

1945

[Invited by Albert Lewin, M.E. enters and wins a competition sponsored by Loew-Lewin for a painting on the theme of *The Temptation of St. Anthony* (cat. no. 100) used in the film *The Private Affairs of Bel Ami*, based on Maupassant's story.]

[Eluard organizes a retrospective exhibition in honor of M.E. at the Galerie Denise René, Paris. Catalogue, bibl. 23.]

1946

Double Wedding in Beverly Hills: M.E. and Dorothea, Man Ray and Juliette Browner. [M.E. and Dorothea Tanning find a temporary retreat in the mountains of Arizona; in Sedona they acquire a piece of land and begin to construct a house. During a stay in the Nevada desert, composes *Sept microbes vus à travers un temperament*, bibl. 19.]

1947

Sedona, Arizona: building, sculpting, painting, writing, and—last (not least) loving (Dorothea).

[*A l'intérieur de la vue—8 poèmes visibles*, poems by Eluard as illustrations to collages by M.E., bibl. 16.]

1948

[*Beyond Painting*, by and about M.E., edited and with an introduction by Robert Motherwell, bibl. 8. M.E. becomes a United States citizen.]

1949

[Retrospective exhibition organized at Copley Galleries,

Lady Bird. 1934-35. Bronze, 20¾″ high. Collection Mr. and Mrs. J. de Menil. Houston.

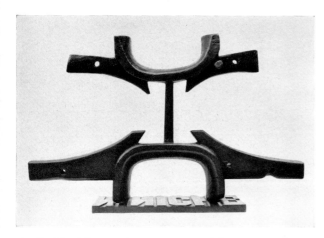

Are You Niniche? 1955-56, Bronze, 22 x 37⅜″.
Collection Mr. and Mrs. Joseph Slifka, New York.

Beverly Hills. On the occasion of the exhibition, the gallery publishes as one volume *At Eye Level/Paramyths*, about and by M.E., bibl. 24. Marcel Duchamp visits Sedona. August: Sails from New Orleans to Antwerp, then by train to Paris.]

With Dorothea saw Paris once more—mixed feelings —Paris and its inhabitants slowly, painfully recovering from Nazi occupation, frustration and disorder.

M.E. was glad to greet his old friends: Arp, Joë Bousquet, Patrick Waldberg, Robert Lebel, André Pieyre de Mandiargues, Georges Bataille, Giacometti, Balthus, Penrose. Also Paul Eluard, in spite of some difficulties (the poet of freedom caught by a merciless discipline.)

[*La Brebis Galante* by Benjamin Péret with illustrations by M.E. published, bibl. 17. The bookstore La Hune, Paris, celebrates the event with a retrospective exhibition of the graphic work of M.E.]

1950

M.E.'s devoted friend, François Victor Hugo, provided

him with a studio on the Quai St. Michel across the river from Notre Dame de Paris.

[Retrospective exhibition organized at the Galerie René Drouin, Paris. Catalogue: preface by Joë Bousquet and text by Michel Tapié, bibl. 25. The exhibition shows, for the first time in Paris, M.E.'s work done in America. October: Returns to Sedona.]

1951

[Loni and Lothar Pretzell, sister and brother-in-law of M.E., organize a large retrospective exhibition at the ruined castle of the archibishops of Cologne at Brühl.] A bolt of lightning destroyed a banner bearing M.E.'s name. This incident considered an omen from the heavens by the inhabitants of the town; the town council met during the night; the exhibition ended with a huge deficit for the city administration and with the disgrace of the very understanding and very well-intentioned *Stadtdirektor*, personally accused of responsibility for the financial disaster. [This exhibition at Brühl, bibl. 26, had considerable influence in the Rhineland, still recovering from Nazi suppression of all modern art.]

1952

[March: Yves Tanguy visits Sedona. During the summer M.E. conducts a course of about thirty lectures at the University of Hawaii, Honolulu. Subject: The last fifty years of modern art. About ninety-six students—corrects their examination papers. Also gives one general lecture on surrealism. In Houston, at the Contemporary Art Association, Dominique de Menil, aided by A. Iolas, organizes an exhibition of M.E.'s work.]

1953

[M.E. returns to Paris. Works in the Impasse Ronsin, next to Brancusi, in a studio lent to him by the painter William Copley. Retrospective exhibition organized by E.L.T. Mesens and P.G. van Hecke (with collaboration

left: *Bosse-de-Nage*. 1959. Bronze, 18⅛″ high. right: *Daughter and Mother*. 1959. Bronze, 17¾″ high. Both Galerie Chalette, New York.

Gypsy Dream Rose. 1959. Bronze, 11⅛″ high. Galerie Chalette, New York.

of the Institute of Contemporary Arts, London) at the Municipal Casino, Knokke-le-Zoute, Belgium; catalogue, bibl. 27. *Das Schnabelpaar*, a poem and eight etchings in color by M.E. published, bibl. 18.]

[Fall: Visits Cologne, the Rhineland and Heidelberg.] M.E. had not seen Cologne for twenty-five years. Naturally it was a terrible shock to him. Nothing remained of the city, every stone of which he had known. When reconstruction of the Town Hall was begun, they found an old Roman villa, perfectly preserved. It was fantastically luxurious, and with a (modern!) system of central heating through the floor.

1954

At the Twenty-seventh Biennale of the City of Venice,

M.E. to his astonishment grabbed first prize.

1955

[Settles in Huismes in Touraine near Chinon. *Galapagos* by Antonin Artaud with illustrations by M.E. published, bibl. 20.]

1956

[At a shop in Chinon finds border strips of old-fashioned wallpapers similar to those he had used more than thirty-five years before and, for his amusement, makes a series of collages: *Dada Forest*, *Dada Sun* (cat. nos. 231-233). Retrospective exhibition organized at the Kunsthalle, Berne, catalogue preface by Franz Meyer, bibl. 28.]

1957

[Winter, 1956-57: Sedona. At the Museum of Tour, an exhibition with Man Ray, Dorothea Tanning and Mies van der Rohe sponsored by Les Services des Relations Culturelles de l'Ambassade des Etats-Unis.]

1958

[Becomes a French citizen. Patrick Waldberg's biography, *Max Ernst*, published, bibl. 30. The bookstore La Hune celebrates the event with an exhibition.]

Spring: M.E. was astonished when he was informed that the Museum of Modern Art in New York wished to organize an exhibition of his work.

1959

[November: A large retrospective exhibition of his work opens at the Musée d'Art Moderne. Catalogue edited by Gabrielle Vienne, preface by Jean Cassou, bibl. 31.]

1960

[Autumn: Trip to Germany with Patrick Waldberg. *Max Ernst* with texts by M.E., preface by Georges Bataille published, bibl. 32.]

1961

January: M.E. arrived in New York with the intention of visiting Sedona, an exhibition at the Museum of Modern Art and, perhaps, his grandchildren. He reread (with interest) this dated data, a chronology unchronologically composed. In it he found things old, things new (and some things censored). It is, he decided, to be read in English by other friends, some new, some old, all young.

MAX ERNST
23 January, 1961
New York

Elephant of the Celebes. 1921. Oil on canvas, 49¼ x 42⅛". Collection Roland Penrose, London.

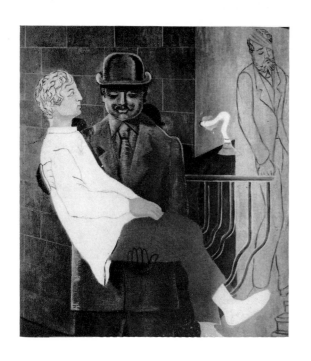

Woman, Old Man and Flower. 1924. Oil on canvas, 38 x 51¼″. The Museum of Modern Art, New York.

OPPOSITE PAGE:

top left: *Revolution by Night.* 1923. Oil on canvas,
45⅝ x 35″. Collection Roland Penrose, London.

top right: *Saint Cecilia.* 1923. Oil on canvas, 39⅜ x
31⅞″. Collection M. H. Franke, Murrhardt, Württemberg.

bottom left: *Equivocal Woman.* 1923. Oil on canvas,
51⅜ x 38⅛″. Collection Mr. and Mrs. Joseph Slifka, New York.

bottom right: *Ubu Imperator.* 1924. Oil on canvas, 38⅜ x 31⅞″.
Collection Mme Hélène Hersaint, Behoust, Seine-et-Oise.

A 100,000 Doves. 1925. Oil on canvas, 31⅞ x 39⅜″. Collection Mme Simone Collinet, Paris.

LEFT, TOP TO BOTTOM:

In Praise of Folly. 1924. Oil on canvas, 7⅞ x 9″.
Collection A. D. Mouradian, Paris.

Labyrinth. 1924. Oil on cardboard, 9 x 7″.
Collection A. D. Mouradian, Paris.

Birds. 1924. Oil on sandpaper, 13⅝ x 11⅝″.
Collection Mr. and Mrs. George S. Rosenthal, Cincinnati.

Birds. 1924. Oil on sandpaper, 13½ x 11⅝″.
Collection S. Tarica, Paris.

top left: *A Very Pretty Forest Stretched Out*. 1925-26. Oil on canvas, 39⅜ x 16¾". Private collection, New York.

top right: *Idol*. 1926. Oil on canvas, 46 x 28¾". Private collection, Paris.

bottom left: *The Doves Are Folded in Their Wings*. 1925. Oil on canvas, 21⅝ x 18⅛". Richard Feigen Gallery, Chicago.

bottom right: *Sun and Forest*. 1926. Oil on canvas, 25⅝ x 21¼". Collection John L. Loeb, Jr., New York.

top left: *The Bride of the Wind*. 1926. Oil on canvas, 32 x 39½".
Collection Dr. and Mrs. Abraham Melamed, Milwaukee.

top right: *The Bride of the Wind*. 1926. Oil on canvas, 25½ x 31¾".
Collection Dr. Henry M. Roland, Woking, Surrey.

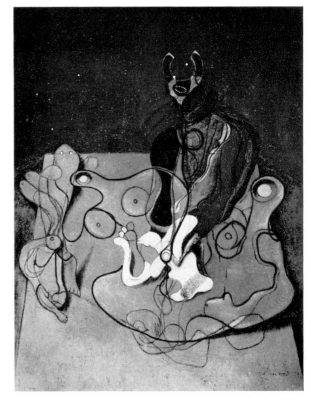

One Night of Love. 1927. Oil on canvas, 64 x 51¼".
Private collection, Paris.

top left: *The Horde*. 1927. Oil on canvas,
18 x 21¾". Roland, Browse & Delbanco,
London.

top right: *Young People Trampling Their Mother*.
1927. Oil on canvas, 18½ x 21⅝".
Collection A. D. Mouradian, Paris.

The Horde. 1927. Oil on canvas, 44⅞ x 57½".
Stedelijk Museum, Amsterdam.

32

The Great Forest. 1927. Oil on canvas, 45⅛ x 57½″.
Kunstmuseum, Basel.

Forest. 1927. Oil on canvas, 44⅞ x 57½″.
Collection Mr. and Mrs. Joseph Slifka, New York.

Vision Provoked by the Nocturnal Aspects of the Porte St. Denis. 1927. Oil on canvas, 25¾ x 32 ″. Collection Marcel Mabille, Brussels.

OPPOSITE PAGE:

far left: *Sun and Forest.* 1926. Oil on canvas, 26 x 32½ ″.
Collection Richard S. Zeisler, New York.

left: *Gray Forest.* 1926. Oil on canvas, 31½ x 39⅜ ″.
Collection Fernand C. Graindorge, Liège.

Monument to Birds. 1927.
Oil on canvas, 64 x 51¼".
Collection Vicomtesse de Noailles,
Paris.

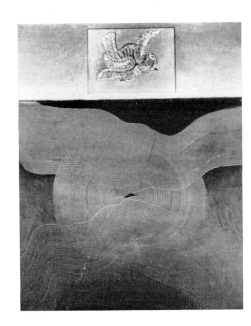

left: *The Gulf Stream*. 1927.
Oil on canvas, 28⅜ x 23¼".
Collection Fernand C. Graindorge, Liège.

far left: *Revolt of the Doves*. 1927.
Oil on canvas, 31½ x 25⅝".
Private collection, Switzerland.

right: *Birds above the Forest*. 1929.
Oil on canvas, 31¾ x 25¼".
The Museum of Modern Art, New York.
Mrs. Katherine S. Dreier Bequest.

far right: *Flower and Animal Head*. 1928.
Oil on canvas, 39¼ x 31¾".
Collection Mr. and Mrs. Arne Horlin
Ekstrom, New York.

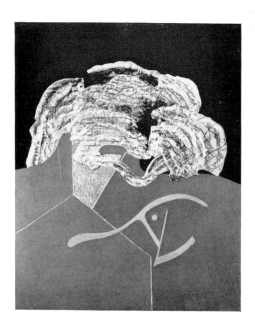

36

right: *Two Anthropomorphic Figures*. 1930.
Oil on canvas, 26 x 21¼".
Collection Mr. and Mrs. Pierre Matisse, New York.

far right: *Figure*. 1931. Painted and
modeled plaster on wood, 72 x 39".
The artist.

left: *The Sea*. 1928. Painted and
modeled plaster on canvas, 22 x 18½".
The Museum of Modern Art,
New York.

far left: *Sea, Sun, Earthquake*. 1931.
Oil on canvas with pasted wallpaper,
28⅝ x 23¾". The artist.

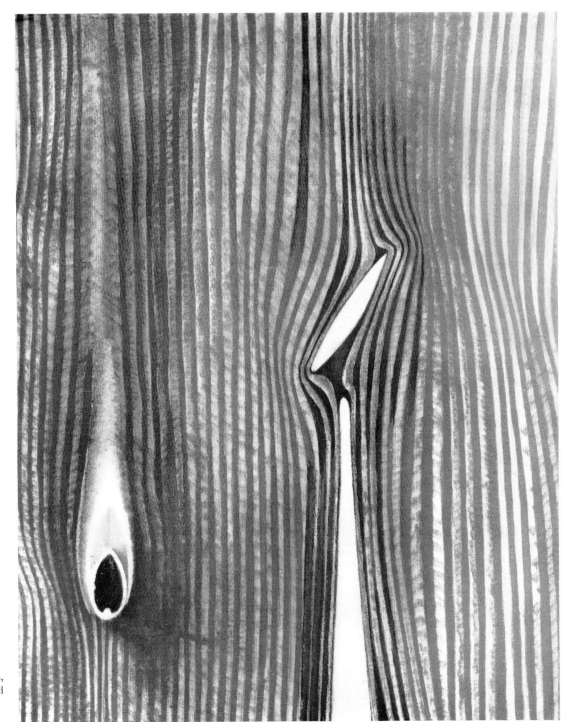

Blind Swimmer. 1934. Oil on canvas, 36¼ x 28⅞″. Collection Mr. and Mrs. Julien Levy, Bridgewater, Connecticut.

Forest. 1933. Oil on canvas, 64 x 100″. Collection Mr. and Mrs. Robert Thurman, Boston.

right: *Garden Airplane Trap.* 1935.
Oil on canvas, 23⅝ x 32″.
Collection Mr. and Mrs. Ernö
Goldfinger, London.

far right: *Garden Airplane Trap.*
1935. Oil on canvas, 21¼ x 29″.
The artist.

The Joy of Living. 1936. Oil on canvas, 28⅝ x 36″. Collection Roland Penrose, London.

far left: *Barbarians Marching to the West.* 1935. Oil on board, 9½ x 13″. Collection Roland Penrose, London.

left: *The Nymph Echo.* 1936. Oil on canvas, 18¼ x 21¾″. The artist.

The Entire City. 1936. Oil on canvas, 38⅛ x 58″. Collection James Ducellier, Carcassonne.

The Entire City. 1935. Oil on canvas, 19¾ x 25⅝″. Private collection, Paris.

A Moment of Calm. 1939. Oil on canvas, 70⅞ x 128″. The artist.

The Angel of Hearth and Home. 1937. Oil on canvas, 44⅞ x 58″. Private collection, Paris.

TOP ROW, LEFT TO RIGHT:

Displaced Person. 1939. Oil on canvas, 13¾ x 10⅝″.
Collection M. and Mme Serge Landeau, Paris.

The Spanish Physician. 1940. Oil on canvas,
24 x 29″. Collection Mr. and Mrs. Joseph R. Shapiro,
Oak Park, Illinois.

Napoleon in the Wilderness. 1941. Oil on canvas,
18¼ x 15″. The Museum of Modern Art, New York.

Totem and Taboo. 1941. Oil on canvas,
28¾ x 36⅜″. Mr. and Mrs. William N. Copley,
Longpont-sur-Orge, Seine-et-Oise.

The Eye of Silence. 1943-44. Oil on canvas,
42½ x 55½″. Washington University, St. Louis.

Europe after the Rain. 1940-1942. Oil on canvas, 21½ x 58⅛″.
Wadsworth Atheneum, Hartford. The Ella Gallup Sumner
and Mary Catlin Sumner Collection.

44

Vox Angelica. 1943. Oil on canvas painted
in four parts, each 30 x 40″.
Collection Mr. and Mrs. Julien Levy,
Bridgewater, Connecticut.

Day and Night. 1941-1942
Oil on canvas, 44¼ x 57½″.
Collection Wright S. Ludington,
Santa Barbara.

OPPOSITE PAGE:

right: *Gardenia.* 1945. Oil on canvas, 25½ x 21⅛″.
Collection M. and Mme Serge Landeau, Paris.

right center: *Euclid.* 1945. Oil on canvas, 25¾ x 23⅝″.
Collection Mr. and Mrs. J. de Menil, Houston.

far right: *Back Fire:* 1950. Oil on canvas, 45¾ x 35″.
The artist.

The Phases of the Night. 1946. Oil on canvas, 36 x 64″. Collection Walter Read Hovey, Pittsburgh.

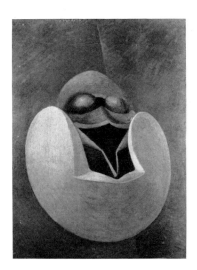

The Polish Rider. 1954.
Oil on canvas, 45¾ x 35″.
Private collection, Paris.

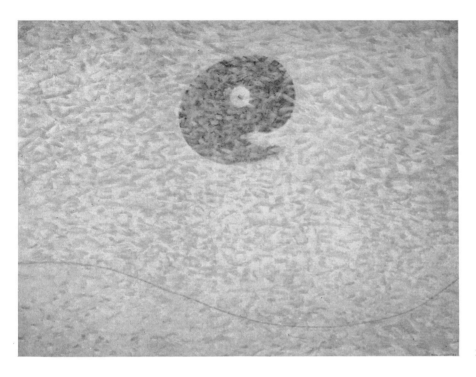

The Cry of the Gull. 1953. Oil on canvas,
37¼ x 51¼″. Collection François de Menil, Houston.

right: *Tomb of the Poet:*
"*After Me Comes Sleep.*" 1958.
Oil on canvas, 25⅝ x 21¼″.
Collection Patrick Waldberg, Paris.

far right: *For D.* 1958.
Oil on wood, 21¾ x 18⅛″
Collection Miss Dorothea Tanning,
Huismes, Indre-et-Loire.

right: *Perched on the Shoulder of a Mocking Angel, Apollo Sings the Praise of Pan.* 1957-58. Oil on canvas, 18 x 14⅛" Collection Mr. and Mrs. Harold X. Weinstein, Chicago.

far right: *Princes Do Not Sleep Well.* 1957. Oil on canvas, 45½ x 35". The Mayor Gallery Ltd., London.

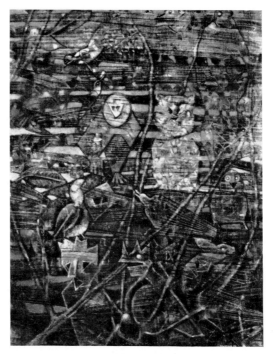

far left: *The Obscure Gods.* 1957. Oil on canvas, 45¾ x 35". Folkwang Museum, Essen.

left: *For Alice's Friends.* 1957. Oil on canvas, 46 x 35½". Private collection, Paris.

Mundus est Fabula. 1959. Oil on canvas, 51 ¼ x 64 ″. The artist.

An Anxious Friend [two views]. 1944. Bronze, 26⅜″ high. Collection Mr. and Mrs. Joseph Slifka, New York.

bottom left: *The King Playing with the Queen.* 1944. Bronze, 38½″ high. The Museum of Modern Art, New York. Gift of Mr. and Mrs. J. de Menil.

bottom right: *Moon Mad.* 1944. Bronze, 36¼″ high. Collection Mr. and Mrs. Joseph Slifka, New York.

CATALOGUE OF THE EXHIBITION

The following catalogue consists of four sections: paintings; sculpture and reliefs; watercolors, drawings, gouaches and collages; portfolios and illustrated books.

The editor has tried to establish the exact location where each work was executed. Although some titles were conceived in English, most often they appear here in translation accompanied by the original German and French. Titles in Latin have not been translated.

In dimensions height precedes width. Works marked with an asterisk are illustrated.

Paintings

1 [Flowers and Fish.] 1916 dated. Oil on canvas, 30 x 24″. Collection Mr. and Mrs. Chaim Gross, New York. [Painted during the war in France.]

2 *Aquis Submersus.* Cologne, 1919. Oil on canvas, 21¼ x 17¼″. Collection Roland Penrose, London.

*3 Elephant of the Celebes. *L'Éléphant Célèbes.* Cologne, 1921 dated. Oil on canvas, 49¼ x 42⅛″. Collection Roland Penrose, London. Ill. p. 25.

*4 *Oedipus Rex.* Cologne, 1922 dated. Oil on canvas, 35 x 45¾″. Private collection, Paris. [The last picture painted by the artist in Cologne.] Ill. p. 13.

5 Earthquake. *Tremblement de terre.* Paris, 1922. Oil on wood, 7½ x 9½″. Collection Mme Simone Collinet, Paris.

*6 Revolution by Night. *La révolution la nuit.* St. Brice, 1923 dated. Oil on canvas, 45⅝ x 35″. Collection Roland Penrose, London. Ill. p. 26.

*7 Equivocal Woman. *Femme Chancelante.* Paris, 1923 dated. Oil on canvas, 51⅜ x 38⅛″. Collection Mr. and Mrs. Joseph Slifka, New York. Ill. p. 26.

*8 Saint Cecilia. *Sainte Cécile (Le piano invisible).* Paris, 1923 dated. Oil on canvas, 39⅜ x 31⅞″. Collection M. H. Franke, Murrhardt, Württemberg. Ill. p. 26.

9 The Couple. *La Couple.* Paris, 1923 dated. Oil and pasted lace-paper on canvas, 8 x 9⅞″. Collection Jacques Ulmann, Paris. [Study for a painting of the same name in a private collection in Belgium.]

*10 *Ubu Imperator.* Paris, 1924. Oil on canvas, 39⅜ x 31⅞″. Collection Mme Hélène Hersaint, Behoust, Seine-et-Oise. Ill. p. 26.

*11 Woman, Old Man and Flower. *Weib, Greis u[nd] Blume.* St. Brice, Paris, Eaubonne, 1924. Oil on canvas, 38 x 51¼″. The Museum of Modern Art, New York. [Begun in 1923, completely repainted in 1924.] Ill. p. 27.

*12 Two Children Are Threatened by a Nightingale. *2 enfants sont menacés par un rossignol.* Eaubonne, 1924. Oil on wood with wood construction, 18 x 13″. The Museum of Modern Art, New York. [Wooden frame by the artist; for a detailed analysis of the painting and its history, see Sidney Janis, bibl. 22, pp. 10-12.] Frontispiece.

13 Sleepwalker. *Noctambule.* Eaubonne, 1924. Oil with painted frame, 7⅛ x 11⅜″. Private collection, Paris.

*14 In Praise of Folly. *Éloge de la Folie.* Paris, 1924. Oil on canvas, 7⅞ x 9″. Collection A. D. Mouradian, Paris. Ill. p. 28.

*15 Labyrinth. *Labyrinthe.* Paris, 1924. Oil on cardboard, 9 x 7″. Collection A. D. Mouradian, Paris. Ill. p. 28.

*16 [Birds] Paris, 1924. Oil on sandpaper, 13⅝ x 11⅝″ including cork frame. Collection Mr. and Mrs. George S. Rosenthal, Cincinnati. [Cork frame by the artist.] Ill. p. 28.

*17 [Birds.] Paris, 1924. Oil on sandpaper, 13½ x 11⅝″ including cork frame. Collection S. Tarica, Paris. [Cork frame by the artist.] Ill. p. 28.

18 [Birds.] Paris, 1924. Oil on sandpaper, 7½ x 11″. Collection Mr. and Mrs. E. A. Bergman, Chicago.

19 [Birds.] Paris, 1924. Oil on wood, 13⅜ x 10½″. Collection A. D. Mouradian, Paris.

*20 A 100,000 Doves. *Aux 100,000 Colombes.* Paris, 1925. Oil on canvas, 31⅞ x 39⅜″. Collection Mme Simone Collinet, Paris. [Aux 100,000 Chemises, then as now, a chain of men's clothiers in Paris.] Ill. p. 28.

*21 The Doves Are Folded in Their Wings. *Colombes s'enfermant dans leurs ailes.* Paris, 1925 dated. Oil on canvas, 21⅝ x 18⅛″. Richard Feigen Gallery, Chicago. Ill. p. 29.

21a The Celestial Army. *L'Armée Céleste.* Paris, 1925. Oil on canvas, 31½ x 39⅜″. Collection Jacques Bolle, Brussels.

*22 A Very Pretty Forest Stretched Out. *Très Jolie Forêt Allongée.* Paris, 1925-26. Oil on canvas, 39⅜ x 16¾″. Private collection, New York. Ill. p. 29.

23 Forest. *Forêt.* Paris, 1925-26. Oil on canvas, 38¼ x 16¼″. Private collection, Paris.

24 Forest and Sun. *Forêt et Soleil.* Paris, 1926. Oil on canvas, 28¾ x 36¼″. The Museum of Modern Art, New York.

*25 Sun and Forest. *Soleil et Forêt.* Paris, 1926. Oil on canvas, 25⅝ x 21¼″. Collection John L. Loeb, Jr., New York. Ill. p. 29.

*26 Idol. *L'Idole.* Paris, 1926 dated. Oil on canvas, 46 x 28¾″. Private collection, Paris. Ill. p. 29.

27 Two Sisters. *Deux Soeurs.* Paris, 1926 dated. Oil on canvas, 39½ x 28¾″. The Museum of Modern Art, New York. Gift of Mme Helena Rubinstein.

28 [Sea.] Paris, 1926. Oil on wood, 13⅛ x 9½″. Collection Mr. and Mrs. Stanley M. Freehling, Highland Park, Illinois.

29 The Wheel of the Sun. *La Roue du Soleil.* Paris, 1926 dated. Oil on canvas, 57¾ x 45⅛″. Private collection, Switzerland.

*30 The Bride of the Wind. *La Mariée du Vent.* Paris, 1926. Oil on canvas, 32 x 39½″. Collection Dr. and Mrs. Abraham Melamed, Milwaukee. Ill. p. 30.

*31 The Bride of the Wind. *La Mariée du Vent.* Paris, 1926. Oil on canvas, 25½ x 31¾″. Collection Dr. Henry M. Roland, Woking, Surrey. [The third and last painted version; the second version listed above; the first version, in a private collection in Switzerland, repr. Cahiers d'Art, bibl. 21, p. 56.] Ill. p. 30.

*32 Gray Forest. *Forêt Grise.* Paris, 1926. Oil on canvas, 31½ x 39⅜″. Collection Fernand C. Graindorge, Liège. Ill. p. 32.

*33 Sun and Forest. *Soleil et Forêt.* Paris, 1926. Oil on canvas, 26 x 32½″. Collection Richard S. Zeisler, New York. Ill. p.32.

34 At the Antipodes of the Landscape. *Aux Antipodes du Paysage.* Paris, 1926. Oil on canvas, 18½ x 21⅝″. Private collection, New York.

*35 Young People Trampling Their Mother. *Jeunes gens piétinant leur mère.* Megève, 1927. Oil on canvas, 18½ x 21⅝″. Collection A. D. Mouradian, Paris. Ill. p. 31.

36 Vision Provoked by a String Found on My Table. *Vision provoquée par une ficelle que j'ai trouvée sur ma table.* Megève, 1927. Oil on canvas, 16⅛ x 13″. Collection Mme Simone Collinet, Paris.

*37 The Horde. Megève, 1927. Oil on canvas, 18 x 21¾″. Roland, Browse & Delbanco, London. Ill. p. 31.

*38 The Horde. *La Horde.* Paris, 1927. Oil on canvas, 44⅞ x 57½″. Stedelijk Museum, Amsterdam. Ill. p. 31.

39 Raft. *Radeau.* Paris, 1927. Oil on canvas, 24 x 31⅞″. Private collection, Paris.

*40 Forest. *Forêt.* Paris, 1927. Oil on canvas, 44⅞ x 57½″. Collection Mr. and Mrs. Joseph Slifka, New York. Ill. p. 32.

*41 The Great Forest. *La Grande Forêt.* Paris, 1927. Oil on canvas, 45⅛ x 57½″. Kunstmuseum, Basel. Ill. p. 32.

*42 Vision Provoked by the Nocturnal Aspects of the Porte St. Denis. *Vision provoquée par l'aspect nocturne de la Porte St. Denis.* Paris, 1927. Oil on canvas, 25¾ x 32″. Collection Marcel Mabille, Brussels. Ill. p. 33.

*43 One Night of Love. *Une nuit d'amour.* Paris, 1927 dated. Oil on canvas, 64 x 51¼″. Private collection, Paris. Ill. p. 30.

*44 The Gulf Stream. *Le Gulf-Stream.* 1927. Oil on canvas, 28⅜ x 23¼″. Collection Fernand C. Graindorge, Liège. Ill. p. 35.

*45 Revolt of the Doves. *La Révolte des Colombes.* Paris, 1927. Oil on canvas, 31½ x 25⅝″. Private collection, Switzerland. Ill. p. 35

46 [Study for Monument to Birds.] Paris, 1927. Oil on composition board, 9½ x 12¾″. Collection Robert Hendrickx, Brussels.

47 [Study for Monument to Birds.] Paris, 1927. Oil on composition board, 9½ x 12⅞″. Richard Feigen Gallery, Chicago.

*48 Monument to Birds. *Monument aux Oiseaux.* Paris, 1927 dated. Oil on canvas, 64 x 51¼″. Collection Vicomtesse de Noailles, Paris. Ill. p. 34.

49 After Us—Motherhood. *Après nous la Maternité.* Paris, 1927. Oil on canvas, 57½ x 45″. The Mayor Gallery Ltd. London.

50 Ridged Forest. *Forêt Arête.* Meudon, 1927-28. Oil on canvas, 10⅝ x 8⅝″. Private collection, Paris.

51 Ridged Forest. *Forêt Arête.* Meudon, 1927-28. Oil on canvas, 10 x 8½″. Collection Mr. and Mrs. Arne Horlin Ekstrom, New York.

52 Drum Flower. *Tambour-Fleur.* Paris, 1928. Oil on canvas, 18⅛ x 15″. Collection S. Tarica, Paris.

53 Shell Flower. *Coquille-Fleur.* Paris, 1928. Oil on canvas, 25⅝ x 21¼″. Philadelphia Museum of Art, The Louise and Walter Arensberg Collection. [This painting is also known as *Sea Shell*.]

*54 Flower and Animal Head. *Fleur—Tête d'animal.* Paris, 1928.

Oil on canvas, 39¼ x 31¾″. Collection Mr. and Mrs. Arne Horlin Ekstrom, New York. Ill. p. 35.

55 Shell Flowers. *Coquille-Fleurs*. Paris, 1928. Oil on canvas, 45½ x 35″. Collection Mr. and Mrs. Leigh B. Block, Chicago.

*56 Birds above the Forest. *Oiseaux au-dessus de la forêt*. Paris, 1929. Oil on canvas, 31¾ x 25¼″. The Museum of Modern Art, New York. Mrs. Katherine S. Dreier Bequest. Ill. p. 35.

57 At the Heart of Sight: The Egg. *A l'intérieur de la vue: L'Oeuf*. Paris, 1929 dated. Oil on canvas, 38¾ x 31¼″. Collection Mr. and Mrs. Robert Thurman, Boston. [The four corners were painted a few years later.]

58 Anthropomorphic Figure. Paris, 1929-30. Oil on composition board, 10¾ x 8¾″. Collection Richard L. Feigen, Chicago.

*59 Two Anthropomorphic Figures. *Deux Figures Anthropomorphes*. Paris, 1930 dated. Oil on canvas, 26 x 21¼″. Collection Mr. and Mrs. Pierre Matisse, New York. Ill. p. 36.

60 Sun in 1900. *Soleil 1900*. Paris, 1930. Oil on canvas with pasted wallpaper, 18⅛ x 15″. Collection Mr. and Mrs. Julien Levy, Bridgewater, Connecticut.

*61 Sea, Sun, Earthquake. *Mer, Soleil, Tremblement de Terre*. Paris, 1931 dated. Oil on canvas with pasted wallpaper, 28⅝ x 23¾″. The artist. Ill. p. 36.

62 Forest and Sun. *Forêt et Soleil*. Paris, 1932. Oil on paper mounted on board, 9 x 12⅛″. Collection Dr. Henry M. Roland, Woking, Surrey.

*63 Forest. *Forêt*. Vigoleno, 1933. Oil on canvas, 64 x 100″. Collection Mr. and Mrs. Robert Thurman, Boston. Ill. p. 38.

64 The Song of the Finch. *Le Chant du Pinson*. Paris, 1933 dated. Oil, crayon and pasted paper on canvas, 32 x 39″. The Bodley Gallery, New York.

65 Spanish Dancer. *Danseuse Espagnole*. Paris, 1934 dated. Oil on canvas, 15 x 11½″. The artist.

*66 Blind Swimmer. *Nageur Aveugle*. Paris, 1934 dated. Oil on canvas, 36¼ x 28⅞″. Collection Mr. and Mrs. Julien Levy, Bridgewater, Connecticut. Ill. p. 37.

67 Blind Swimmer. *Nageur Aveugle*. Paris, 1934 dated. Oil on canvas, 36¼ x 28¾″. Collection Mr. and Mrs. Pierre Matisse, New York.

68 Garden Airplane Trap. *Jardin Gobe-Avions*. Paris, 1935. Oil on canvas, 15 x 21⅜″. Collection Mr. and Mrs. Kurt Seligmann, Sugar Loaf, New York.

*69 Garden Airplane Trap. *Jardin Gobe-Avions*. Paris, 1935 dated. Oil on canvas, 21¼ x 29″. The artist. Ill. p. 38.

*70 Garden Airplane Trap. *Jardin Gobe-Avions*. Paris, 1935. Oil on canvas, 23⅝ x 32″. Collection Mr. and Mrs. Ernö Goldfinger, London. Ill. p. 38.

71 Garden Airplane Trap. *Jardin Gobe-Avions*. Paris, 1935. Oil on canvas, 15 x 21⅜″. Private collection, Paris.

72 Garden Airplane Trap. *Jardin Gobe-Avions*. Paris, 1935. Oil on canvas, 18⅛ x 24″. Collection Bernard Penrose, Cornwall.

73 Barbarians Marching to the West. *Barbares marchant vers l'ouest*. Paris, 1935 dated. Oil on paper mounted on board, 9⅛ x 12″. Collection Mr. and Mrs. Harold X. Weinstein, Chicago.

*74 Barbarians Marching to the West. *Barbares marchant vers l'ouest*. Paris, 1935. Oil on board, 9½ x 13″. Collection Roland Penrose, London. Ill. p. 39.

*75 The Entire City. *La Ville Entière*. Paris, 1935. Oil on canvas, 19¾ x 25⅝″. Private collection, Paris. Ill. p. 40.

75a The Entire City. *La Ville Entière*. Paris, 1935-36. Oil on canvas, 23½ x 31½″. Collection Eric Estorick, London.

*76 The Entire City. *La Ville Entière*. 1936 dated. Oil on canvas, 38⅛ x 58″. Collection James Ducellier, Carcassonne. Ill. p. 40.

77 Picnic on the Grass. *Déjeuner sur l'herbe*. 1936 dated. Oil on canvas, 17¾ x 21⅝″. Collection Roland Penrose, London.

78 Nature at Dawn. *La nature à l'aurore*. Paris, 1936. Oil on canvas, 9⅞ x 13¾″. Private collection, Paris.

*79 The Nymph Echo. *La nymphe Écho*. Paris, 1936 dated. Oil on canvas, 18¼ x 21¾″. The artist. Ill. p. 39.

80 The Nymph Echo. *La nymphe Écho*. Paris, 1936 dated. Oil on canvas, 18¼ x 21¾″. The Museum of Modern Art, New York.

*81 The Joy of Living. *La Joie de Vivre*. Paris, 1936 dated. Oil on canvas, 28⅝ x 36″. Collection Roland Penrose, London. Ill. p. 39.

*82 The Angel of Hearth and Home. *L'Ange du Foyer*. Paris, 1937 dated. Oil on canvas, 44⅞ x 58″. Private collection, Paris. Ill. p. 41.

83 Nature at Dawn. *La nature à l'aurore*. Paris, 1938 dated. Oil on canvas, 31⅞ x 39⅜″. The Museum of Modern Art, New York. Gift of Samuel A. Berger.

*84 A Moment of Calm. *Un peu de calme*. Saint Martin d'Ardèche, 1939 dated. Oil on canvas, 70⅞ x 128″. The artist. Ill. p. 41.

*85 Displaced Person. *Apatride*. Les Milles, 1939 dated. Oil on canvas, 13¾ x 10″). Collection M. and Mme Serge Landeau, Paris. [A self portrait, inscribed on verso: *Apatride observé au Camp des Milles*.] Ill. p. 42.

86 [Untitled painting.] Saint Martin d'Ardèche, 1940 dated. Oil on canvas, 8¾ x 6⅜ ". Collection Mr. and Mrs. Varian Fry, Ridgefield, Connecticut.

87 The Painter's Daughters. Saint Martin d'Ardèche, 1940. Oil on canvas, 29 x 24 ". Collection Mr. and Mrs. Bernard J. Reis, New York.

*88 The Spanish Physician. Saint Martin d'Ardèche, 1940. Oil on canvas, 24 x 29 ". Collection Mr. and Mrs. Joseph R. Shapiro, Oak Park, Illinois. Ill. p. 42.

89 The Fascinating Cypress. Le Fascinant Cyprès. Saint Martin d'Ardèche, 1940. Oil on canvas. Private collection, Paris.

*90 Europe after the Rain. L'Europe après la Pluie. Saint Martin d'Ardèche, 1940/New York, 1942 dated. Oil on canvas, 21½ x 58⅛ ". Wadsworth Atheneum, Hartford. The Ella Gallup Sumner and Mary Catlin Sumner Collection. Ill. p. 43.

*91 Napoleon in the Wilderness. Santa Monica, 1941. Oil on canvas, 18¼ x 15 ". The Museum of Modern Art, New York. Ill. p. 42.

*92 Totem and Taboo. Santa Monica, 1941 dated. Oil on canvas, 28¾ x 36⅜ ". Collection Mr. and Mrs. William N. Copley, Longpont-sur-Orge, Seine-et-Oise. Ill. p. 43.

93 Alice in 1941. Santa Monica, 1941 dated. Oil on canvas, 15¾ x 12½ ". Collection James Thrall Soby, New Canaan, Connecticut.

*94 Day and Night. Saint Martin d'Ardèche, 1941/New York, 1942 dated. Oil on canvas, 44¼ x 57½ ". Collection Wright S. Ludington, Santa Barbara. Ill. p. 44.

95 Surrealism and Painting. New York, 1942 dated. Oil on canvas, 76¾ x 91¾ ". Collection Mr. and Mrs. William N. Copley, Longpont-sur-Orge, Seine-et-Oise.

*96 Vox Angelica. Sedona, 1943 dated. Oil on canvas painted in four parts, each 30 x 40 ". Collection Mr. and Mrs. Julien Levy, Bridgewater, Connecticut. Ill. p. 44.

97 Summer Night in Arizona. Sedona, 1943. Oil on canvas, 11 x 17 ". Collection Mr. and Mrs. Julien Levy, Bridgewater, Connecticut.

*98 The Eye of Silence. New York, 1943-44 dated. Oil on canvas, 42½ x 55½ ". Washington University, St. Louis. Ill. p. 43.

99 Arizona Night. New York, 1944 dated. Oil on canvas, 14⅛ x 22 ". Collection Mr. and Mrs. Julien Levy, Brigewater, Connecticut.

100 The Temptation of Saint Anthony. New York, 1945 dated. Oil on canvas, 43⅜ x 50⅞ ". Private collection, Paris.

*101 Gardenia. New York, 1945 dated. Oil on canvas, 25½ x 21⅛ ". Collection M. and Mme Serge Landeau, Paris. Ill. p. 45.

*102 Euclid. New York, 1945 dated. Oil on canvas, 25¾ x 23⅝ ". Collection Mr. and Mrs. J. de Menil, Houston. Ill. p. 45.

103 Rhenish Night. La Nuit Rhénane. New York, 1945. Oil on canvas, 51¼ x 63 ". Private collection, Paris.

*104 The Phases of the Night. Sedona, 1946 dated. Oil on canvas, 36 x 64 ". Collection Walter Read Hovey, Pittsburgh. Ill. p. 45.

105 [Study for Feast of the Gods.] Sedona, 1948 dated. Oil on canvas, 20⅛ x 20 ". Collection Mr. and Mrs. E. A. Bergman, Chicago.

106 Feast of the Gods. Le Régal des Dieux. 1948 dated. Oil on canvas, 60 x 42 ". Collection Jacques Ulmann, Paris.

107 Wind and Space. Sedona, 1948 dated. Oil on canvas, 10 x 40 ". Collection Miss Dorothea Tanning, Huismes, Indre-et-Loire.

108 Head of a Bull. Sedona, 1948 dated. Oil on canvas, 18 x 16 ". Collection Mr. and Mrs. Julien Levy, Bridgewater, Connecticut.

109 Inspired Hillock. Colline Inspirée. Paris, 1949 dated. Oil on canvas, 15 x 18¼ ". Private collection, Paris.

*110 Back Fire. Retour de Flamme. 1950 dated. Oil on canvas, 45¾ x 35 ". The artist. Ill. p. 45.

111 The Portuguese Nun. La Réligieuse Portugaise. Paris, 1950 dated. Oil on canvas, 45¾ x 35 ". Mme Hélène Hersaint, Behoust, Seine-et-Oise.

112 Here Everybody Speaks Latin. Paris, 1950 dated. Oil on canvas, 39⅝ x 25¾ ". Collection Miss Philippa de Menil, Houston.

113 Arizona. Sedona, 1952. Oil on composition board, 10 x 5 ". Collection Marechal Brown, Villanova, Pennsylvania.

114 Hawaii. Sedona, 1952. Oil on composition board, 10 x 5 ". Collection Marechal Brown, Villanova, Pennsylvania.

115 The Painter's Palette. La Palette du Peinture. Paris, 1953. Oil on canvas, 35 x 45¾ ". Collection Maurice Lefebvre-Foinet, Paris.

116 Colorado of Medusa. Coloradeau de Méduse. Paris, 1953 dated. Oil on canvas, 28¾ x 36¼ ". Collection Maurice Lefebvre-Foinet, Paris.

*117 The Cry of the Gull. Le Cri de la Mouette. Paris, 1953 dated. Oil on canvas, 37¼ x 51¼ ". Collection François de Menil, Houston. Ill. p. 47.

118 The Song of the Frog. *Le Chant de la Grenouille.* Paris, 1953. Oil on canvas, 25¾ x 36¼″. Collection Dieter Keller, Stuttgart-Feuerbach, Germany.

*119 The Polish Rider. *Le Cavalier Polonais.* 1954 dated. Oil on canvas, 45¾ x 35″. Private collection, Paris. Ill. p. 46.

120 Savonarola. *Savonarole.* Paris, 1955. Oil on wood, 8½ x 12½″. Collection Dr. Henry M. Roland, Woking, Surrey.

121 A Remorseless Soul. Huismes, 1955 dated. Oil on canvas, 12 x 10⅛″. Private collection, Paris.

122 Comédia del'Arte. Huismes, 1955 dated. Oil on canvas, 8¾ x 10⅝″. Private collection, Paris.

123 Three Flowers for D. *Trois Fleurs pour D.* Huismes, 1956. Oil on wood, 15⅛ x 18¼″. Collection Miss Dorothea Tanning, Huismes, Indre-et-Loire. [Inscribed: *à Dorothea: mon amour my love*].

124 Project for a Monument to Leonardo da Vinci. *Project pour un monument à Léonard de Vinci.* Huismes, 1956. Oil on canvas, 14 x 11⅜″. Collection M. and Mme Serge Landeau, Paris.

125 Leonardo da Vinci. Huismes, 1956 dated. Oil on wood, 6¼ x 4¾″. Collection Miss Dorothea Tanning, Huismes, Indre-et-Loire.

126 Moon-Fish. *Poisson-Lune.* Huismes, 1956 dated. Oil on wood, 10⅝ x 8¾″. Collection M. and Mme Serge Landeau, Paris.

127 My Name Is If and No. Sedona, 1957 dated. Oil on canvas, 15 x 14″. Collection Marechal Brown, Villanova, Pennsylvania.

128 Quasimodo Genetis. Sedona, 1957. Oil on canvas, 24 x 18″. Collection Alexander Margulies, London.

129 The Childhood of Art. *L'Enfance de l'Art.* 1957. Oil on wood, 16¼ x 13″. Collection Mme Jean Riboud, Paris.

*130 For Alice's Friends. *Pour les amis d'Alice.* Huismes, 1957 dated. Oil on canvas, 46 x 35½″. Private collection, Paris. Ill. p. 48.

131 Sign for a School for Gulls. *Enseigne pour une École des Mouettes.* 1957 dated. Oil on canvas, 44⅞ x 63″. Private collection, Paris.

*132 Princes Do Not Sleep Well. *Les Princes Dorment Mal.* Huismes, 1957 dated. Oil on canvas, 45½ x 35″. The Mayor Gallery Ltd., London. Ill. p. 48.

*133 The Obscure Gods. *Les Dieux Obscurs.* Huismes, 1957 dated. Oil on canvas, 45¾ x 35″. Folkwang Museum, Essen. Ill. p. 48.

134 W. C. Fields. Huisms, 1957. Oil, 6¼ x 4¾″. Collection Patrick Waldberg, Paris.

135 Thirty-three Little Girls Leave to Hunt the White Butterfly. *Trente-trois fillettes partant pour la chasse au papillon blanc.* 1957 dated. Oil on canvas, 39⅜ x 28¾″. Collection Baron Léon Lambert, Brussels.

136 The Good-Natured Crows. *Corbeaux de Bonne Humeur.* Huisms, 1957-58. Oil on canvas, 35 x 51¼″. Collection Georges de Menil, Cambridge, Massachusetts.

*137 Perched on the Shoulder of a Mocking Angel, Apollo Sings the Praise of Pan. *Perché sur l'épaule d'un Ange Moqueur, Apollon chante la louange de Pan.* Huisms, 1957-58. Oil on canvas, 18 x 14⅞″. Collection Mr. and Mrs. Harold X. Weinstein, Chicago. Ill. p. 48.

*138 For D. *Pour D.* 1948. Oil on wood, 21¾ x 18⅛″. Collection Miss Dorothea Tanning, Huismes, Indre-et-Loire. Ill. p. 47. [One of a series of pictures which the artist has painted each year for his wife Dorothea Tanning and which incorporates the initial of her first name.]

139 Winter in Manhattan. Huisms, 1958 dated. Oil on wood, 21⅝ x 17⅞″. Private collection, New York.

*140 Tomb of the Poet: "After Me Comes Sleep." *Tombeau du Poète: "Après moi le sommeil."* Huisms, 1958 dated. Oil on canvas, 25⅝ x 21¼″. Collection Patrick Waldberg, Paris. [A homage to Paul Eluard, and study for the painting in the collection of the artist.] Ill. p. 47.

*141 Mundus est Fabula. Paris, 1959 dated. Oil on canvas, 51¼ x 64″. The artist. Ill. p. 49.

142 Slumbering Sirens. *Les Sirènes s'endorment.* Huisms, 1960 Oil, 25⅝ x 21¼″. Collection Galerie der Spiegel, Cologne

143 Explosion in a Cathedral. *Explosion dans une Cathédrale.* Huisms, 1960 dated. Oil on canvas, 51¼ x 76⅝″. Private collection, Paris.

144 A Swarm of Bees in a Palace of Justice. *Un essaim d'abeilles dans un Palais de Justice.* Huisms, 1960 dated. Oil on canvas, 51⅛ x 76⅝″. Private collection, Paris.

145 Portrait of Dorothea. *Portrait de Dorothea.* Huisms, 1960 dated. Oil on canvas, 63¾ x 51½″. The artist.

Sculpture and Reliefs

146 Dadaville. Paris, 1923-24. Partially painted cork and plaster, 26 x 22″. Collection Roland Penrose, London.

147 [Untitled sculpture]. Paris, 1927. Painted and modeled plaster, 24⅜ x 20⅛″. Collection Mr. and Mrs. William N. Copley, Longpont-sur-Orge, Seine-et-Oise.

148 Doves. *Colombes.* Paris, 1927. Painted and modeled plaster, 8½ x 9″. Collection Mr. and Mrs. William N. Copley, Long-pont-sur-Orge, Seine-et-Oise.

*149 The Sea. *La Mer.* Paris, 1928. Painted and modeled plaster on canvas, 22 x 18½″. The Museum of Modern Art, New York. Ill. p. 36.

*150 Figure. *Figure Humaine.* Paris, 1931 dated. Painted and modeled plaster on wood, 72 x 39″. The artist. Ill. p. 36.

151 Oedipus. *Oedipe.* Paris, 1934 plaster; 1960 bronze. Bronze, 24⅜″ high. The artist.

152 Oedipus [variant]. *Oedipe.* Paris, 1934 plaster; 1960 bronze. Bronze, 25½″ high. The artist.

153 [Untitled sculpture]. Majola, 1934. Painted stone. Private collection, New York.

154 [Untitled sculpture]. Majola, 1934. Painted stone. Collection Mr. and Mrs. Ernö Goldfinger, London.

*155 Lady Bird. *Femme Oiseau.* Paris, 1934-35 plaster; 1950 [?] bronze. Bronze, 20¾″ high. Collection Mr. and Mrs. J. de Menil, Houston. Ill. p. 21.

156 Lunar Asparagus. *Les asperges de la lune.* Paris, 1935. Plaster, 65¼″ high. The Museum of Modern Art, New York.

157 *La Belle Allemande.* Paris, 1935 plaster; 1956 bronze. Bronze, 24″ high. Collection Mr. and Mrs. J. de Menil, Houston.

158 Gay. *Gai.* Paris, 1935 plaster; 1956 bronze. Bronze, 15″ high. Collection Mr. and Mrs. Joseph Slifka, New York.

159 Lady Flower. *Femme Fleur.* Great River, Long Island, 1944 plaster; 1950[?] bronze. Bronze, 14″ high. Private collection, New York.

*160 The King Playing with the Queen. *Le Roi jouant avec la Reine.* Great River, Long Island, 1944 plaster; 1954 bronze. Bronze, 38½″ high. The Museum of Modern Art, New York. Gift of Mr. and Mrs. J. de Menil. Ill. p. 50.

161 Moon Mad. *Moonmad.* Great River, Long Island, 1944. Mahogany, 36¼″ high. Collection Mr. and Mrs. Julien Levy, Bridgewater, Connecticut.

*162 Moon Mad. *Moonmad.* 1944. Bronze, 36¼″ high. Collection Mr. and Mrs. Joseph Slifka, New York. Ill. p. 50.

*163 An Anxious Friend. Great River, Long Island, 1944 plaster; 1950[?] bronze. Bronze, 26⅜″ high. Collection Mr. and Mrs. Joseph Slifka, New York. Ill. p. 50.

164 [Untitled sculpture]. Great River, Long Island, 1944. Plaster, 11″ high. Collection Mr. and Mrs. Bernard J. Reis, New York.

165 The Table Is Set. *Table Mise.* Great River, Long Island, 1944; 1950[?] bronze. Bronze, 11″ high. Collection Mr. and Mrs. J. de Menil, Houston.

166 Two Times One. *Deux Font Un.* Huismes, 1955 bronze; painted 1960. Bronze painted grey, 11¾″ high. The artist.

*167 Are You Niniche? *Etes-vous Niniche?* Huismes, 1955-56. Bronze, 22 x 37⅜″. Collection Mr. and Mrs. Joseph Slifka, New York. Ill. p. 22.

*168 Daughter and Mother. *Fille et Mère.* Huismes, 1959. Bronze, 17¾″ high. Galerie Chalette, New York. Ill. p. 23.

*169 Gypsy Dream Rose. *Gipsy Dreamrose.* Huismes, 1959. Bronze, 11⅛″ high. Galerie Chalette, New York. Ill. p. 23.

*170 *Bosse-de-Nage Réssuscite.* Huismes, 1959. Bronze, 18⅞″ high. Galerie Chalette, New York. [The title refers to Alfred Jarry's talkative character.] Ill. p. 23.

171 Trophy. *Trophée.* Huismes, 1960. Bronze, 10¼″ high. The artist.

172 A Chinaman Fargone. *Un Chinois Egaré.* Huismes, 1960. Bronze, 30¼″ high. The artist.

173 The Spirit of the Bastille. *Le Génie de la Bastille.* Huismes, 1960. Bronze, 123¼″ high. The artist.

Watercolors, Drawings, Gouaches, Collages

174 [Battle of Fish.] 1917 dated. Watercolor, 11⅞ x 7⅞″. Collection M. H. Franke, Murrhardt, Württemberg.

175 [Landscape.] 1917 dated. Watercolor, 7⅞ x 11⅞″. Collection M. H. Franke, Murrhardt, Württemberg.

176 Farewell My Beautiful Land of Marie Laurencin. Help! Help! Inscribed: *Adieu mon beau pays de Marie Laurencin. Hilfe! Hilfe!* Cologne, 1919. Rough proof from assembled printer's plates, altered with pen and ink, 11½ x 5⅝″. The Museum of Modern Art, New York. [Executed on the same day as *Trophy Hypertrophied,* below, while the artist waited in a printer's shop for proofs of a DADA publication. The title, according to the

artist, probably refers to Marie Laurencin's efforts to help him obtain a French visa.]

177 Trophy Hypertrophied. Cologne, 1919. Rough proof from assembled printer's plates, altered with ink, 13⅞ x 7⅛". The Museum of Modern Art, New York, gift of Tristan Tzara. [Rejected by the Section d'Or exhibition, Paris, 1920, because the drawing incorporated printed fragments and, therefore, could not be considered handmade.]

178 Self-constructed Small Machine. Cologne, 1919. Pencil and frottage from assembled printer's plates, 18 x 12". Collection Mr. and Mrs. E. A. Bergman, Chicago. Inscribed: *Selbstkonstruiertes maschinchen in diesem verrührt er meersalat leitartikel leidtragende und eisensamen in zylindern aus bestem mutterkorn sodass vorne die entwicklung und rückwärts die anatomie zu sehen ist der preis stellt sich dann um 4 mark höher. / Petit machine construite par lui-même il y mélange la salade de mer la sperme de fer le périsperme amer d'un côté nous voyons l'évolution de l'autre l'anatomie ça conte 2 sous plus cher.* [Self-constructed small machine in which he mixes sea salad, editorial, mourner, and iron sperm into cylinders of the best ergot so that the development can be seen in front and the anatomy in back. The price is then about 4 marks higher./A little machine constructed by himself, in which he mixes sea salad, iron sperm, bitter perisperm. On one side we see the evolution; on the other, the anatomy. It costs 2 cents more.]

*179 The Roaring of the Ferocious Soldiers (You Who Pass—Pray for DADA). Inscribed: *Le mugissement des féroces soldats/ vous qui passez, priez pour DADA.* Cologne, 1919. Rough proof from assembled printer's plates altered with pen and ink, 14⅛ x 9⅜" [sight]. The Bodley Gallery, New York. Ill. p. 12.

180 Stamens and Marseillaise. Inscribed: *Étamines et Marseillaise.* Cologne, 1919 dated. Rough proof from assembled printer's plates, altered with pencil, gouache, ink, 11⅞ x 9⅞" maximum dimensions. Collection Mr. and Mrs. Kurt Seligmann, Sugar Loaf, New York.

181 Here Everything Is Still Floating. Cologne, 1920. Pasted photoengravings, 4⅛ x 4⅞". The Museum of Modern Art, New York. Inscribed: *Hier ist noch alles in der schwebe. Fatagaga: Le troisième tableau gazométrique.* [Here everything is still floating. Fatagaga: The third gasometric picture.] Jean Arp and the artist collaborated on the series of Fatagaga collages. Here the title was provided by Arp.

182 The Dissolvable Snail. Cologne, 1920 dated. Technical engraving altered with watercolor, 9¼ x 6⅜". Collection Mme Simone Collinet, Paris. Inscribed: *Le limaçon de chambre fusible et le coeur de la moissonneuse légère à la course. Stubenschnecke 5 nummern wandervogel 8 nummern summa 13 nummern sursum corda.* [The

dissolvable snail and the heart of the swift-running harvestress. Snail 5 numbers bird of passage 8 numbers summa 13 numbers sursum corda.]

183 Stratified Rocks. Cologne, 1920. Anatomical engraving altered with gouache and pencil, 6 x 8⅛". The Museum of Modern Art, New York. Inscribed: *Schichtgestein naturgabe aus gneis lava isländisch moos 2 sorten lungenkraut 2 sorten dammriss herzgewächsee b) dasselbe in fein poliertem kästchen etwas teurer.* [Stratified rocks, nature's gift of gneiss, lava, Iceland moss, 2 kinds of lungwort, 2 kinds of ruptures of the perinaeum growths of the heart. b) The same thing in a well polished little box somewhat more expensive.]

184 Above the Clouds Midnight Passes. Cologne, 1920 dated. Pasted photoengravings and pencil, 7¼ x 5⅛". Private collection, New York. Title, not inscribed: *Au dessus des nuages marche la minuit. Au dessus de la minuit plane l'oiseau invisible du jour. Un peu plus haut que l'oiseau l'éther pousse et les murs et les toits flottent.* [Above the clouds midnight passes. Above midnight hovers the invisible bird of day. Still higher than the bird the ether expands and walls and roofs are floating.]

185 The Hat Makes the Man. Cologne, 1920. Pasted papers, pencil, ink, watercolor, 14 x 18". The Museum of Modern Art, New York. Inscribed: *Bedecktsamiger stapel-mensch nacktsamiger wasserformer ("edelformer") kleidsame nervatur auch umpressnerven! (C'est le chapeau qui fait l'homme, le style c'est le tailleur).* [Seed-covered stacked-up man, seedless waterformer, ("edelformer"), well-fitting nervous system also tightly-fitted nerves! (The hat makes the man, style is the tailor.)]

186 The Little Tear Gland That Says Tic Tac. Inscribed: *La petite fistule lacrimale qui dit tic tac.* Cologne, 1920 dated. Wallpaper borders altered with gouache, 14¼ x 10". The Museum of Modern Art, New York. [Formerly collection André Breton, who received it as a gift from the artist. It is the point of departure for several of the artist's paintings such as his series of Forests.]

187 Glacial Landscapes. Cologne, 1920. Wallpaper altered with gouache and pencil, 9⅞ x 6¼". Collection Mme Simone Collinet, Paris. Inscribed: *Eislandschaften eiszapfen u. gesteinsarten des weibl. körper.* [Glacial landscapes icicles and rocks like feminine bodies.]

188 Undulating Katharina. Cologne, 1920 dated. Wallpaper altered with gouache and pencil, 11¾ x 9⅞". Collection Roland Penrose, London. Inscribed: *Katharina ondulata d.i. frau wirtin a.d. Lahn erscheint als der deutschen engelin u. perlmutter auf korksohlen im tierbild des krebses.* [Undulating Katharina—that is, the innkeeper's wife on the River Lahn—appears as the angel

of the Germans and mother-of-pearl on cork soles under the sign of Cancer.]

*189 The Swan Is Very Peaceful. Cologne, 1920. Pasted photo-engravings, 3¼ x 4¾". Collection Mrs. Alfred H. Barr, Jr., New York. Full title, not inscribed: *C'est déjà la vingt-deuxième fois que Lohengrin a abandonné sa fiancée (pour la première fois)/c'est là que la terre a tendu son écorce sur quatre violons/ nous ne nous reverrons jamais/nous ne combattrons jamais contre les anges/le cynge est bien paisible/il fait force de rames pour arriver chez Léda.* [It is already the twenty-second time that (for the first time) Lohengrin has left his fiancée/it is there that the earth has spread its crust on four violins/we will never see each other again/we will never fight against the angels/the Swan is very peaceful/he vows hard to catch Leda.] Ill. p. 11.

190 The Horse, He's Sick. *Un peu malade, le cheval.* Cologne, 1920. Pasted papers, pencil, ink, 5¾ x 8½". The Museum of Modern Art, New York. [This and at least one other collage are related to the painting *La Belle Saison*, 1925, in a private collection in Belgium.]

191 The Sandworm Which Reties. Cologne, 1920. Pasted papers and watercolor, 4½ x 20⅛". Collection Roland Penrose, London. Inscribed: *L'ascaride de sable qui rattache sa sandale/la mouche torpille qui forme un aparté/les terribles lèvres solaires qui s'enroulent autour de l'horizon.* [The sandworm which reties its sandal/the torpedo fly which forms an aside/the terrible solar lips which coil around the horizon.]

192 The Massacre of the Innocents. Inscribed: *Le Massacre des Innocents.* Cologne, 1920. Photomontage, watercolor and pastel, 8¼ x 11½". Collection Mme Simone Collinet, Paris.

193 The Cormorants . . . *Les Cormorans* . . . Cologne, 1920 dated. Pasted papers, 6⅛ x 5⅛". Collection Mme Simone Collinet, Paris.

194 The Cormorants. . . *Les Cormorans* . . . Cologne, 1920 dated. Photomontage, 11½ x 9". Collection Mme Simone Collinet, Paris.

*195 [Untitled collage.] Cologne, 1920. Pasted photoengravings, 2⅜ x 5⅝". Private collection, New York. Ill. p. 11.

*196 Vanity Fair. Cologne, 1920. Pasted photograph altered with gouache and ink, 5⅞ x 4⅛" [sight]. Collection Morris Philipson, New York.

197 Young Chimera. *Jeune Chimère.* Cologne, 1920. Pasted paper and watercolor, 10⅝ x 3⅞". Collection Mme Simone Collinet, Paris. [Study for the painting of the same title in the collection of A. D. Mouradian, Paris.]

198 Two Ambiguous Figures. Cologne, c. 1920. Pasted papers and gouache, 9⅝ x 6¾". Collection Jean Arp, Meudon, Seine-et-Oise. Inscribed: *1 kupferblech 1 zinkblech 1 gummituch 2 tastzirkel 1 abflussfernrohr 1 röhrender mensch.* [1 copper plate, 1 zinc plate, 1 rubber towel, 2 calipers, 1 drainpipe-telescope, 1 roaring man.]

199 The Gramineous Bicycle. Cologne, c. 1920-1921. Botanical chart altered with gouache, 29¼ x 39¼". The Museum of Modern Art, New York. Inscribed: *La bicyclette graminée garnie de grelots les grisous grivelés et les échinodermes courbants l'échine pour quêter des caresses.* [The gramineous bicycle garnished with bells, dappled fire damps and echinoderms who bend their spines to look for caresses.]

200 Winter Landscape. Cologne, 1921 dated. Technical engraving altered with gouache, 5¼ x 8⅛". Collection Jean Arp, Meudon, Seine-et-Oise. Inscribed: *Winterlandschaft: vergasung der vulkanisierten eisenbraut zur erzeugung der nötigen bettwärme* [Winter Landscape: The asphyxiation of the vulcanized iron maiden in order to produce the necessary warmth for the bed.]

201 [Untitled drawing.] Paris, 1923. Ink, 10⅝ x 7⅞" [sight]. Collection A. D. Mouradian, Paris. [Study for *La Belle Jardinière*, destroyed, formerly in the collection of Düsseldorf Museum.]

202 [Untitled drawing.] Paris, 1923. Ink, 5 x 4½" [sight]. Collection A. D. Mouradian, Paris.

203 [Untitled drawing.] Paris, 1924 dated. Ink, 10¾ x 8¼". Collection Allan Frumkin, Chicago.

204 The Earth as Seen from the Earth. *La Terre vue de la Terre.* Pornic, 1925. Pencil frottage, 7½ x 6½". Collection Georges de Menil, Cambridge, Massachusetts.

*205 Earthquake. *Tremblement de Terre.* Pornic, 1925. Pencil frottage, 28½ x 24". The Bodley Gallery, New York. Ill. p. 14.

206 The Sea Rises, as Does the Moon. *La mer se lève, la lune aussi.* Pornic, 1925. Pencil frottage, 7 x 8½". Collection Mr. and Mrs. Harold X. Weinstein, Chicago.

207 The Sap Rises, Rises. *La sève monte, monte.* Pornic, 1925 dated. Pencil frottage, 8¼ x 6⅜". Private collection, New York.

208 The Planet Sheds Its Leaves. Inscribed: *La planète s'effeuille.* Pornic, 1925. Pencil frottage, 8⅜ x 6⅝". Collection John Torson, New York.

209 Flashes of Lightning under Fourteen Years. *Les éclairs au-dessous de quatorze ans.* Pornic, 1925. Pencil frottage, 15¾ x 9⅞". Collection A. D. Mouradian, Paris. [Although cat. nos. 204-209 are from the series *Histoire Naturelle*, only the last was published.]

210 Forest, Sun, Birds. *Forêt, soleil, oiseaux.* Paris, 1928-29. Gouache, 25⅛ x 19⅛″ [sight]. The Museum of Modern Art, New York. Gift of Mme Helena Rubenstein.

*211 Loplop Introduces. *Loplop présente.* Paris, 1929-30. Pasted color engraving and pencil, 24½ x 19″. Collection Mr. and Mrs. E. A. Bergman, Chicago. Ill. p. 16.

212 Loplop Introduces. *Loplop présente.* Paris, 1931. Pasted paper, pencil, pencil frottage, and watercolor, 25⅛ x 19⅜″ [sight]. Collection Mr. and Mrs. Julien Levy, Bridgewater, Connecticut.

213 Loplop Introduces. *Loplop présente.* Paris, 1931. Pencil, pasted engraving, and pasted blotter with ink, 25⅝ x 21¼″. Collection Mr. and Mrs. Ernö Goldfinger, London.

214 Loplop Introduces. *Loplop présente.* Paris, 1931. Pencil, pencil frottage, and embossed cardboard pasted on paper, 25 x 19½″ [sight]. Collection Mr. and Mrs. Julien Levy, Bridgewater, Connecticut.

215 Loplop Introduces. *Loplop présente.* Paris, 1931. Pasted marble paper, pencil, and lithograph altered with pencil, 19⅜ x 25¼″. Collection Mr. and Mrs. Julien Levy, Bridgewater, Connecticut.

*216 Loplop Introduces. *Loplop présente.* Paris, 1931. Pasted paper, pencil, and crayon, 25⅜ x 19⅝″. Collection Mr. and Mrs. Julien Levy, Bridgewater, Connecticut. Ill. p. 16.

217 Hand and Butterflies. *Main et papillons.* Paris, 1931. Pasted paper, 18 x 25½″. Private collection, New York.

218 Loplop and the Butterflies. *Loplop aux papillons.* Paris, 1932 dated. Pencil and pasted paper, 25¼ x 31″. Wadsworth Atheneum, Hartford. The Ella Gallup Sumner and Mary Catlin Sumner Collection.

218a Loplop Introduces. *Loplop présente.* Paris, 1932 dated. Pasted paper, watercolor and pencil, 19⅝ x 25⅜″. Collection Mr. and Mrs. E. A. Bergman, Chicago.

219 Birds. *Les Oiseaux.* Paris, 1932. Gouache, 14 x 9⅜″ [sight]. Collection Mr. and Mrs. Julien Levy, Bridgewater, Connecticut.

220 [Sun and Forest]. Paris, 1932. Oil on paper, 9¾ x 14″. Collection Mr. and Mrs. David M. Solinger, New York.

221 Sun over the Sea. Paris, 1932. Gouache, 9⅝ x 13⅞″ [sight]. Collection Dr. and Mrs. Allan Roos, San Francisco.

*222 Study for the stage set for *Ubu Enchaîné*, Paris, 1937. Pasted engravings, pencil and colored crayon, 9⅝ x 13¼″. The Bodley Gallery, New York. [This and cat. no. 223 and 224 are studies for a production of Alfred Jarry's play.] Ill. p. 19.

223 Study for the stage set for *Ubu Enchaîné.* Paris, 1937. Pasted engravings, pencil and colored crayon, 9⅝ x 13¼″. Collection Mr. and Mrs. Joseph R. Shapiro, Oak Park, Illinois.

224 Study for the stage set for *Ubu Enchaîné.* Paris, 1937. Pasted engravings, pencil and colored crayon, 9⅝ x 13¼″. Collection Mr. and Mrs. Joseph R. Shapiro, Oak Park, Illinois.

225 Displaced Man. *Apatride.* Les Milles, 1939 dated. Pencil and pencil frottage, 7¾ x 5″. Private collection, New York.

226 Displaced Woman. *Apatride.* Les Milles, 1939 dated. Pencil and pencil frottage, 7¾ x 6″. Private collection, New York.

227 [Untitled drawing.] New York, 1942. Crayon heightened with white chalk on orange paper, 17¾ x 13¾″. Collection Mr. and Mrs. E. A. Bergman, Chicago.

228 [Untitled drawing.] New York, 1942. Pencil, heightened with white chalk on orange paper, 18⅞ x 12⅛″. Collection Mr. and Mrs. Julien Levy, Bridgewater, Connecticut.

229 [Skull.] Arizona, 1949 dated. Pasted engravings and ink, 8⅝ x 6⅞″ [sight]. The Bodley Gallery, New York. [This and cat. no. 230 are from a series of eleven drawings for an unpublished text by Joë Bousquet entitled *Absolument ou le vide à l'envers.* See bibl. 25.]

230 [Bat.] Arizona, 1949 dated. Pasted engravings and ink, 8¾ x 7″ [sight]. The Bodley Gallery, New York.

231 Dada Sun, Dada Forest. *Soleil dada, forêt dada.* Huismes, 1956. Pasted wallpaper and engravings, c. 24 x 15″. The artist.

232 Dada Sun, Dada Forest. *Soleil dada, forêt dada.* Huismes, 1956. Collage, 15½ x 11″. Collection Patrick Waldberg, Paris.

233 Dada Sun, Dada Sea. *Soleil dada, mer dada.* Huismes, 1956. Oil and pasted paper, 23½ x 18½″. Collection Judge and Mrs. Henry Epstein, New York.

Portfolios and Illustrated Books

234 *Fiat Modes Pereat Ars*. 1919. A portfolio of eight lithographs, 17⅛ x 12″ each. The Museum of Modern Art, New York.

*235 Paul Eluard, *Répétitions*. 1922. Reproductions of eleven collages, see bibl. 11. The Museum of Modern Art, New York. Gift of Walter P. Chrysler, Jr. Ill. p. 13.

236 Book plate for Paul Eluard. c. 1925. Lithograph, 3⅛ x 2½″. The Museum of Modern Art, New York. Gift of Walter P. Chrysler, Jr.

237 *Histoire Naturelle*. 1926. A portfolio of thirty-four phototype reproductions of pencil frottages of 1925, see bibl. 12. The Museum of Modern Art, New York. Gift of James Thrall Soby.

238 *La Femme 100 Têtes*. 1929. Reproductions of 149 collages, see bibl. 13. The Museum of Modern Art, New York. Gift of Walter P. Chrysler, Jr.

239 *Une Semaine de Bonté, ou les Sept éléments capitaux*. 1934. Five volumes containing reproductions of 188 collages, see bibl. 15. The Museum of Modern Art, New York. Gift of Walter P. Chrysler, Jr.

240 Benjamin Péret, *La Brebis Galante*. 1949. Illustrated with etchings in color as well as reproductions of collages, see bibl. 17. Exhibited: the etched title page, 9⅜ x 7½″, collection The Museum of Modern Art, New York; one of the original collages, 11½ x 8⅞″, collection Mr. and Mrs. Raymond J. Braun, New York; and a frottage, 9⅝ x 15¼″, from the engraved plate used to reproduce it, collection David Mann, New York.

SELECTED BIBLIOGRAPHY

This list represents a suggestive cross section from the international commentary of forty years. Widespread references will be found in numerous journals, such as *La Révolution Surréaliste* and *Littérature* in Paris, along with *View* and *VVV* in New York, most pre-eminently in *Cahiers d'Art* and most currently in *XXe Siècle*. Existing documentation (e.g. bibl. 21, 22, 26, 29, 32, 41, 48), will draw fuller attention to material both by and about Max Ernst, including, of course, his extensive graphic work (bibl. 37, 45). The chronologies are incorporated into bibl. 29, 31, 46. The selection below should be viewed in relation to bibliographies previously published by this compiler in 1948 (bibl. 8) and in 1951 (bibl. 44).

Bernard Karpel, Librarian of the Museum

Major Texts by the Artist

1 Vom Werden der Farbe. *Der Sturm* 8 no. 5:66-68 Aug. 1917.

2 Visions de demi-sommeil. *La Révolution Surréaliste* no. 9-10:7 Oct. 1, 1927.

3 Comment on force l'inspiration. *Le Surréalisme au Service de la Révolution* no. 6 May 15, 1933.
   "Extraits du traité de la peinture surréaliste." For translations as "Inspiration to order" see: *This Quarter* Sept. 1932; *The Painter's Object*, ed. by M. Evans (London, Howe, 1937); *The Creative Process*, ed. by B. Ghiselin (Berkeley & Los Angeles, Univ. of California, 1952), *Beyond Painting* (bibl. 8).

4 Les mystères de la forêt. *Minotaure* no. 5-6 May 1934.

5 Was ist Surrealismus? p. 3-7 *In* ZURICH. KUNSTHAUS. Ausstellung. Oct.-Nov. 1934.
   Republished in bibl. 26.

6 Au delà de la peinture. *Cahiers d'Art* no. 6-7 1936.
   Also in special number (bibl. 21). Translated in bibl. 8.

7 Préface, ou Loplop présente la mariée du vent. *In* LEONORA CARRINGTON. La Maison de la Peur. p [1-2] Paris, Parisot, 1938.

8 Beyond Painting, and Other Writings by the Artist and His Friends. New York, Wittenborn, Schultz, 1948.
   Edited by Robert Motherwell. Includes: Beyond painting.—Inspiration to order.—Some data on the youth of M. E. Essays by Arp, Breton, Calas, Levy, Matta, Ribemont-Dessaignes; bibliography of 164 references by B. Karpel.

9 Notice biographique rédigée par l'artist. *In* Max Ernst [Catalogue]. Paris, Musée d'Art Moderne, Nov.-Dec. 1959.

SEE ALSO: bibl. 12 (Berggruen), 14, 18, 22, 26, 32, 50, 53, 54, 57, 60.

Selected Graphic Editions

For complete and more recent checklists see Edwards (bibl. 37), Seghers (bibl. 32) and, most comprehensively, Nicaise (bibl. 45).

10 Les Malheurs des Immortels. Paris, Librairie Six, 1922.
   "Révélés par Paul Eluard et Max Ernst." American edition: New York, Black Sun Press, 1943.—German edition: Cologne, Galerie der Spiegel, 1960.

11 Répétitions. Dessins de Max Ernst. Paris, Au Sans Pareil, 1922. Text by Paul Eluard.

12 Histoire Naturelle. Paris, Éditions Jeanne Bucher, 1926.
   Frottages, issued loose in folio; introduction by Arp (reprinted bibl. 34). Another edition issued by Pauvert (Paris, 1960). Smaller frottages from the same series (1925) published as: *Histoire Naturelle. Dessins Inédits*. Paris, Berggruen [1959?]. A plaquette in reduced format, with introduction by the artist. Original edition (1926) reproduced in miniature in bibl. 26.

13 La Femme 100 Têtes. Paris, Éditions du Carrefour, 1929.
   Collages; "avis au lecteur" by André Breton. Reprint: Éditions de l'Oeil, 1956 (American distributor: George Wittenborn, N. Y.).

14 Rêve d'une Petite Fille qui Voulut Entrer au Carmel. Paris, Éditions du Carrefour, 1930.
   Prefatory text and captions for 80 collages.

15 Une Semaine de Bonté, ou Les Sept Éléments Capitaux: Roman. Paris, Éditions Jeanne Bucher, 1934.
   Collages; boxed set of five parts. Perhaps the most symphonic statement in this distinctive form.

16 A l'Intérieur de la Vue—8 Poèmes Visibles. Paris, Seghers, 1947.
   39 illustrations by Ernst (1931), with poems by Eluard (1946).

17 La Brebis Galante. Paris, Éditions Premières, 1949.
   Text by Benjamin Péret, with color etchings and drawings in color.

18 Das Schnabelpaar. Basel, Ernst Beyeler, 1953.
   Eight color etchings and "ein Gedicht."

19 Sept Microbes, Vus à Travers un Temperament. Paris, Cercle des Arts, 1953.
   Color reproductions (same size as the original miniatures). New edition: Cologne, Galerie der Spiegel, 1957.

20 Galapagos—Les Iles du Bout du Monde. Paris, Broder, 1955.
   Text by Antonin Artaud; 10 etchings and cover collage. Also reported as : Éditions Thésée (Paris, 1954).

Monographs and Catalogues

21 ZERVOS, CHRISTIAN, ed. Max Ernst: Oeuvres de 1919 à 1936. Paris, Éditions Cahiers d'Art, 1937.
   Special number of *Cahiers d'Art*. Texts by Breton, Crevel, Desnos, Hugnet, Tzara, etc. Numerous illustrations; bibliography.

22 VIEW. [Max Ernst Number]. New York, 1942.
   Special issue of the magazine, 2nd series, no. 1, with bibliography. Texts by Breton, Calas, Carrington, Ernst, Janis, Miller, Ozenfant, Tyler. Catalogue of exhibit at Valentine Gallery, Mar. 23-Apr. 11, 1942.

23 RENÉ, DENISE, GALERIE. Max Ernst. Paris, 1945.
   Checklist of June exhibit of 38 works (1919-1937). Poems by Eluard and Hugnet.

24 COPLEY GALLERIES. Max Ernst, 30 Years of His Work, a Survey. Beverly Hills, Cal., 1949.
   Catalogue of 66 works (1919-1948) for Jan. 10-Feb. 20 exhibit. Cover title: Ernst At Eye Level/Paramyths. Includes supplemental section (Paramyths) "designed by Max Ernst."

25 DROUIN, RENÉ, GALERIE. Max Ernst: Textes de Joë Bousquet et Michel Tapié. Paris, René Drouin, 1950.
   Includes "11 dessins de Max Ernst"; lists 64 works; also limited edition.

26 PRETZELL, LOTHAR & PRETZELL, LONI, ed. Max Ernst: Gemälde und Graphik, 1920-1950. [Stuttgart, Kohlhammer, 1952.]
   Commemorative illustrated booklet issued after the summer 1951 anniversary exhibit in Brühl (Schloss Augustusberg). Texts by Arp, Ernst, and others; bibliography. Includes as insert the 1951 catalogue listing the 158 exhibits at Brühl. Also modified showings elsewhere in Germany, e.g. Mannheim Kunsthalle, Jan. 6-Feb. 3, 1952.

27 KNOKKE LE ZOUTE. ALBERT PLAGE. CASINO COMMUNAL. Max Ernst. Brussels, Éditions de la Connaissance, 1953.
   Exhibit held July 4-Aug. 30; organized by E.L.T. Mesens and P. G. van Hecke with collaboration of the Institute of Contemporary Arts, London. Catalogue, by Mesens, includes 83 works with annotations.

28 BERNE. KUNSTHALLE. Max Ernst. Berne, 1956.
   Preface by Franz Meyer; chronology; lists 89 works (12 plates); held Aug. 11-Sept. 15.

29 TRIER, EDUARD. Max Ernst. Cologne, Seemann, 1956.
   References, p. 30. In the series: Monographien zur Rheinisch-Westfälischen Kunst der Gegenwart, no 11 issued with updated chronology by Verlag Bongers, Recklinghausen, 1959.

30 WALDBERG, PATRICK. Max Ernst. Paris, Pauvert, 1958.
   The major illustrated monograph; 443 p., numerous plates.

31 PARIS. MUSÉE D'ART MODERNE. Max Ernst. Paris, Éditions des Musées Nationaux, 1959.
   Biographical chronology edited by the artist; preface by J. Cassou; catalogue by G. Vienne; 175 works shown Nov. 13-Dec. 31.

32 SEGHERS, PIERRE, ed. Max Ernst. Paris, Gonthier-Seghers, 1959.
   "Texte inédit" by Ernst; preface by G. Bataille; critiques and bibliography (including graphic editions). Collection "Propos et Présence," no. 3.

33 HOMMAGES À MAX ERNST. Cologne, Galerie der Spiegel, 1960.
   Texts—some previously published—by Arp, Bosquet, Bousquet, Eluard, Magritte, Michaux, Péret, Waldberg.

General References

34 ARP, HANS. Onze Peintres Vus par Arp. Zurich, Girsberger, 1949.
   "Introduction à l'Histoire naturelle de Max Ernst" (p. 38-41). From bibl. 12; reprinted bibl. 26.

35 BARR, ALFRED H., JR. Fantastic Art, Dada, Surrealism. Essays by Georges Hugnet. 3 ed. New York, Museum of Modern Art, 1946.
   First edition for exhibition of 1936, with catalogue. General bibliography and important chronology.

36 BRETON, ANDRÉ. Les Pas Perdus. Paris, Gallimard, 1924.
   Commentary (p. 101-3, 147, 156-8, 196) continued in his: *Le Surréalisme et la Peinture* (Paris, Gallimard, 1928; N. Y., Brentano's, 1945), and later works.

37 EDWARDS, HUGH. Surrealism and Its Affinities. Chicago, Art Institute of Chicago, 1956.
   "The Mary Reynolds collection, a bibliography."

38 GIEDION-WELCKER, CAROLA. Contemporary Sculpture. New York, Wittenborn, 1955.
   Includes biographical and bibliographical notes. Also German edition (Gerd Hatje Verlag).

39 GUGGENHEIM, PEGGY. Confessions of an Art Addict. New York, Macmillan, 1960.
> Previously published: Art of This Century (N. Y., Art of This Century, 1942).—Out of This Century (N. Y., Dial, 1946).

40 HUGNET, GEORGES. L'Aventure Dada (1916-1922). Paris, Galerie de l'Institut, 1957.
> Introduction by T. Tzara. Also text in bibl. 35, 44.

41 HUYGHE, RENÉ, ed. Histoire de l'Art Contemporain: la Peinture Paris, Alcan, 1935.
> Reprint of L'Amour de l'Art (Mar. 1934) with texts by R. Huyghe and J. Cassou; bibliography by G. Bazin.

42 JANIS, SIDNEY. Abstract and Surrealist Art in America. New York, Reynal & Hitchcock, 1944.

43 JEAN, RENÉ. History of Surrealist Painting. New York, Grove, 1960.
> With the collaboration of Arpad Mezei. Extensive references to Ernst. First edition (382 p.): Paris, Éditions du Seuil, 1959.

43a LOOKING AT MODERN PAINTING. Los Angeles, University of California, 1957.
> Surrealist section by F. S. Wight on Woman, Old Man and Flower (Museum of Modern Art); biographical note.

44 MOTHERWELL, ROBERT, ed. The Dada Painters and Poets: an Anthology. New York, Wittenborn, Schultz, 1951.
> Comprehensive collection of documents and essays including Hugnet's "L'esprit dada" from Cahiers d'Art. Extensive bibliography by B. Karpel; detailed Ernst references (p. 358, 379, 384).

45 NICAISE, LIBRAIRIE. [Catalogue No. 10]: Cubisme, Futurisme, Dada, Surréalisme. Paris, 1960.
> Detailed inventory of texts and editions-de-luxe including 39 Ernst citations. For similar documentary coverage: Surréalisme, Poésie et Art contemporaine (Paris, Matarasso, 1949).

46 RAYNAL, MAURICE [& OTHERS]. History of Modern Painting, [Vol. 3]: From Picasso to Surrealism. Geneva, Skira, 1950.
> Includes chronology and bibliography. Also, in one vol. ed.: Modern Painting (1953, 1956).

47 RITCHIE, ANDREW C., ed. German Art of the Twentieth Century by Werner Haftmann, Alfred Hentzen, William S. Lieberman. New York, Museum of Modern Art, 1957.
> For exhibition with the St. Louis Museum; works by and data on Ernst, including graphics; bibliography.

48 VOLLMER, HANS. Allgemeines Lexikon der bildenden Künstler des XX Jahrhunderts. v. 2, p. 52 Leipzig, Seemann, 1955.
> With bibliography.

Recent Articles

49 BOSQUET, ALAIN. Le bonheur de Max Ernst, Quadrum (Brussels) no. 5, 1958.
> English summary (p. 187).

50 CABANNE, PIERRE. Max Ernst. Arts (Paris) no. 793 Oct. 26-Nov. 1, 1960.
> A history, evaluation and interview; quotes Ernst, p. 16.

51 CONNOLLY, CYRIL. Surrealism. Art News (N. Y.) Nov. 1951.
> A survey article in its 1952 annual number.

52 DUPIN, JACQUES. Les dernières peintures de Max Ernst. Cahiers d'Art (Paris) 28, no. 1, 1953.

53 ERNST, MAX. Souvenirs rhénans. L'Oeil no. 16 Apr. 1956.
> Recollections of early days and friends.

54 JOUFFROY, ALAIN. Max Ernst, un indépendant . . . Arts (Paris) no. 537 Oct. 1955.
> Also Kunsten Idag (Oslo) no. 4 1959 (with French translation) and an interview (Arts, no. 756, Jan. 1960).

55 PIERRE DE MANDIARGUES, ANDRÉ. Max Ernst. Art International (Zurich) 4 no. 1 1960.
> French text also in I 4 Soli (Venice) Jul.-Aug. 1959.

56 RICHTER, HANS. Max Ernst. La Biennale di Venezia no. 19-20 Apr.-June 1960.
> Also: À propos de Max Ernst et de "La Semaine de Bonté" Style en France (Paris) no. 4, 1946.

57 SCHUSTER, JEAN. Interview with Max Ernst sur l'Allemagne. Medium no. 2 Feb. 1954.
> On the postwar situation.

58 SOLIER, RENÉ DE. Papiers collés surréalistes. XXe Siècle (Paris) no. 6 Jan. 1956.
> All illustrations by Ernst; text from unpublished work on the artist.

59 SPIELMANN, HEINZ. Notizen über Max Ernst und Herkules Seghers. Das Kunstwerk (Baden-Baden) no. 8 Feb. 1960.
> With French and English summary.

60 SWEENEY, JAMES JOHNSON. Eleven Europeans in America: [Max Ernst]. Museum of Modern Art Bulletin, no. 4-5 1946.
> Interview with chronology and bibliography.

61 WALDBERG, PATRICK. [Max Ernst] Cahiers d'Art (Paris) no. 2 1949.
> Also essays on the artist appearing variously in Mercure de France (no. 1126, 1957), XXe Siècle (Paris) no. 8, Jan. 1957, and no. 10 and no. 11, 1958. For monograph, see bibl. 30.